Glad Reunion

Other Books by John Claypool

Tracks of a Fellow Struggler
Stages: The Art of Living the Expected
The Preaching Event: The Lyman Beecher Lectures
The Light Within You: Looking at Life Through New Eyes
Opening Blind Eyes

GLAD REUNION

Meeting Ourselves in the Lives of Bible Men and Women

John Claypool

WORD BOOKS
PUBLISHER
WACO, TEXAS

A DIVISION OF
WORD, INCORPORATED

GLAD REUNION: MEETING OURSELVES IN THE LIVES
OF BIBLE MEN AND WOMEN

Library of Congress Cataloging in Publication Data:

Claypool, John.
   Glad reunion.

   1. Bible.   O.T. — Biography.   I. Title.
BS571.C495   1985   221.9'22   85-5362
ISBN 0-8499-0469-2

Printed in the United States of America

To my mother and father,
Mary Etta Buchanan Claypool
and
John Rowan Claypool III,
who gave me the gift of life
and
the encouragement always to make
the most of it

Contents

INTRODUCTION

QUITE A FEW YEARS ago now, when my children were still small, we spent one Thanksgiving attending a family reunion at the farm in southern Kentucky where members of my family had lived for seven generations. The house that stands there now is an enlargement of the log cabin in which my grandfather and his mother before him were born. As was usual at such get-togethers, there was lots of reminiscing going on, and I noted with interest the response of my two little ones. They sat spellbound for hours as different kinspersons recounted tales out of our family heritage.

It suddenly struck me that what was going on in that moment was of primal significance for my children's development. They were reconnecting with their roots long before any of us had heard of Alex Haley, and in the process they were developing a stronger, more vital sense of who they were. Carlyle Marney has suggested that there are at least eighty thousand generations behind each one of us, and that we are incapable of blessing ourselves or giving blessing to others until first we are able to bless our own origins. "The stuff God had at His disposal in creating us"—this is what we need first to learn about and understand, then to accept, and finally to bless. This was the process my little ones were beginning around that Thanksgiving table at the family farm. They were becoming aware of that vast and ambiguous background out of which they had sprung and over against which they were going to have to forge out their own identities. Marney calls this process "going through home again," and I see it as a crucial part of the maturing process.

I have come to believe that what is true in a physical-family
sense is also true in a religious sense; that is, in order to
understand ourselves as the people of God, we need to look
back across the centuries to all that lies behind us. And this,
of course, is where the Old Testament fits so beautifully into
the scheme of things, for the Old Testament is to the church
what that farm in southern Kentucky was to my particular
family—namely, a place of remembrance, a repository of history and tradition. It can even be thought of as a family
scrapbook in which pictures and memorabilia of the past
are preserved. The Old Testament is where we get in touch
with our religious root system, and this is as important to
our faith as family stories are to a particular family heritage.

It was in this sense, then, that I decided to explore some
of the pivotal persons in the Old Testament under the general
theme of "glad reunion." I felt that it would serve a significant
purpose for all of us to become better acquainted with some
of our ancestors of the Old Testament in the same way that
my children had come to know stories about "Grandpa" and
"Lynn" and some of the other landmark lives on the Claypool
family tree. It was in this way that the idea for this volume
was born.

I have used many of the thoughts contained in the pages
to follow in sermons to at least four different congregations.
I have also added material of late out of my own growing
awareness that our "foremothers" are as important to our
heritage as our forefathers. Several of the men and women
who had interacted with me over this material have encour-
aged me to give it the more permanent form of "bookhood,"
and I am indebted to all those persons, as well as to Floyd
Thatcher and Word Publishers for enabling me to come to
this point of gift giving. I am also indebted once again to
the inspired and careful editing of Anne Christian Buchanan.
Her efforts on behalf of my book *The Light Within You* made
it a much better volume, and I now acknowledge that the
same is true of these pages.

On the personal side, let me acknowledge a special debt
of gratitude to the many secretarial colleagues who had a
hand in preparing this material. Most recently, Marie Wil-
liams and Genny Campbell in Lubbock have been most gen-
erous with their time and creative abilities. Without their

collaboration, this task would have been much later in coming to its present form.

Walter Shurden, a noted Baptist historian who now teaches at Mercer University, said recently in my hearing, "Tell me what you remember and I will tell you who you are." I think that insight is eminently correct. Memory is a crucial component of personal identity. It is my hope that this volume will contribute to a better sense in all of us of that "goodness and mercy that have been following us all the days of our lives." I gladly now release these words into the mysterious wind of the Holy Spirit to be scattered and used as that One sees fit. My highest hope would be that these words would effect a kind of "glad reunion" with our spiritual family akin to the good times I shall always remember gratefully around that Thanksgiving table in southern Kentucky.

John R. Claypool

1

ABRAHAM
Dynamic Security

PERHAPS THE BEST PLACE to begin our journey of "glad re-union" with our biblical family is with the man who has been called "our father in faith"—the patriarch Abraham. It is with him that Old Testament history really begins.

You may already be familiar with the broad outlines of Abraham's life. The first time we see him in the book of Genesis (Gen. 11:26), he is living in southern Mesopotamia as a part of the Chaldean/Babylonian culture. Subsequently, his whole clan moved north to Haran, and there the most formative event of his life occurred; God himself encountered Abraham and made him a most extraordinary promise: a land to call his own, descendants more numerous than the sands of the sea, a name that would resound throughout history, and—best of all—a means by which all the families of the earth could bless themselves.

To receive all this, Abraham was asked to do only one thing—leave where he was and set out on a journey which Yahweh promised to direct step by step. "The Lord will provide"—these four words were to become the foundation of the whole enterprise, and Abraham is depicted as responding to this beckoning without a word of question or argument. He left Haran and began a journey that never really ended. Abraham and his family moved first to Palestine and then to Egypt and then back again to Palestine where he moved around constantly until Isaac, the son the Lord had promised him, was finally born. Only near the end of his life did Abraham finally buy a parcel of ground in which to bury his wife and later himself.

In broad generalities, these are the facts about our father Abraham. However, if this is all we know about him, the real value he can have for our experience will be missed. There are lessons we can learn from Abraham when we move behind the facts and see the whole canvas of his life. I have gained a certain "feel" for life by watching Abraham do what he did, and I would like to point out three ways in which Abraham's experience can be enriching for all of us.

The first thing I have learned from Abraham is that God's kind of security is dynamic, not static. If there is one word that sums up Abraham's experience with God, it is the word *movement.* Instead of giving this man something to hang onto, a secure anchor that would hold steady amid all changes, Yahweh gave him a call to adventure and a promise to provide for him as he went. "Get thee up from this place and go to the place that I will show you," is the gist of what Yahweh said to Abraham—not just once at the beginning (Gen. 12:1), but all through his life. There was no settling down or "nesting in" with this deity. He was forever on the move—that seems to be the essence of his reality.

Jürgen Moltmann has pointed to this dynamic character as the distinguishing feature of biblical religion. Pagan religions—or "epiphany religions" as he calls them—center on creating stability in the midst of chaos. They attempt to establish a condition of permanence in time and space. This is the very opposite of what Moltmann calls the "exodus religion" of Abraham, which regards change and movement not as enemies to be resisted, but as *ways God does his work and calls human beings to fulfillment.* Security with this kind of God never means sitting still or possessing something or remaining static; it means being continually on the way to some goal beyond the present that beckons but is as yet unattained. The symbol of this kind of religion would be a hoisted sail, not an anchor; the goal is "a promised land" out ahead, not a haven of rest.

When you stop and think about it, this is a seminal insight into the nature of existence itself. It affects the way one relates to that most basic of all realities—the reality of change.

Let's face it: the only thing in life that does *not* change is the fact of change itself. Like it or not, we all have to cope with the flux inherent in all things.

What Abraham's experience teaches me is that such change is the way God does his work, not an obstacle to it. It relieves me from the utterly futile attempt to freeze time or try to establish permanence, and it gives me the courage to step out in the confidence that "the Lord will provide" as the way unfolds. That really is the only kind of security that is possible in our kind of world, is it not? Where nothing stays the same for long—not our bodies or our ideas or our families or anything—to see security in terms of permanence is folly indeed. But to be told, "as your days, so will your strength be," in other words, as you change, what you have to have will be provided—that is realistic. And Abraham's whole life is a confirmation that this is true and can be trusted and lived out as he most assuredly did.

The second thing I have learned from Abraham is a theme I never tire of emphasizing—that perfection is not a prerequisite for God to begin his work with an individual. What we see here at the very beginning of the history of faith is crucially important. God really is willing to take us where we are and patiently to move us toward where he wants us to be. Perfection rightly belongs at the *end* of the process of God's dealing with us, not at the beginning or even in the middle.

This fact becomes so clear in the Abraham saga. Although this man did manifest heroic qualities of faith and trust at the start of his life, he was by no means "finished" or "completed" in a personal sense. As an old black preacher once put it: "There were parts of him that had not yet heard the Word." Abraham was as capable of mistrust and fearfulness as he was of faith and courage, and several times we see him falling and failing, even after the process of promise had begun.

For example, soon after he had arrived in Palestine and been told that this was indeed the land of promise, a famine arose. Abraham became frightened and took things into his own hands, fleeing unbidden into Egypt, where he thought there was more food. Under the threat of starvation, his faith in God's power to provide melted like a block of ice on the Fourth of July. And once he got to Egypt, his fears got the best of him again, and he asked his wife, Sarah, to do an incredible thing. She was apparently a very beautiful woman, and Abraham became afraid that some Egyptian prince would see her, want her, and have Abraham killed because he was her husband. So he proposed to Sarah that if this should occur, she should claim to be Abraham's sister. If necessary, she should even go and marry such a prince so that Abraham's skin might be saved! Any way you look at it, this was a shabby, self-serving performance, and one which God himself had to step in and untangle.

The point I am making is that Abraham was by no means perfect at any point in his life. Yet God worked with him nonetheless and moved him slowly and mercifully toward perfection.

This is such a needed perspective for many of us—that perfection rightly belongs at the *end* of God's dealing with us, not at the beginning or in the middle of the process. It is the goal toward which we strive, the norm by which we measure our progress, but it is not something that we must have in order for God to love us, nor is it something we can expect to embody fully at any stage of our human journey.

I have often thought of the generations who would have been helped if the last verse in the fifth chapter of Matthew had been translated differently. We are all familiar with the King James version of that verse: "Be ye therefore perfect, even as your Father which is in heaven is perfect" (Matt. 5:48). But in the original Greek, the imperative ("be ye") and the future ("ye shall") are spelled the same way. Had that translation been "*Ye shall* be perfect, even as your Father in heaven is perfect"—that is, put in the form of gracious promise—I believe it would have been much closer to the truth of the whole biblical religion and perhaps saved us from the notion that perfection is what we must do on our own in order to qualify for God's love.

What we see in the experience of Abraham is that he was moved step by step toward perfection by a love that was willing to begin with him where he was and to grow him from there. I can think of no insight that could free and liberate us more fully than the recognition that God is patient with growing things, that he is no stranger to chaos and incompleteness, and that he is willing and able to work with us "through our stuff" toward a more perfect day.

The third insight I have gained from Abraham's story is

that *life is to be regarded as gift*—every last particle of it. This realization has been particularly meaningful in my own life. It was some fifteen years ago now, on a Saturday afternoon in January, that my little daughter, Laura Lue, moved into "the valley of the shadow of death" after a dreadful struggle with leukemia. Interestingly enough, it was an experience out of Abraham's life that helped me more than anything else to get through that night of grief. I am referring now to his being called to offer up his son, Isaac (Gen. 22:1–19).

I had always had a problem with this whole story until a German interpreter named Gerhard Von Rad opened up its deeper meaning for me. He pointed out that the command to go to Mount Moriah and sacrifice Isaac was not a regression into the paganism in which Abraham had grown up; it was Yahweh's way of finding out whether Abraham really had gotten the point after all of these years of living with the Lord's wonderful promises. The whole thing had started for Abraham just as his life had; it was something given to him without any question of his deserving it. He had done nothing to earn or merit this offer of a land and descendants and fame and the chance to bless all subsequent generations. It was all "windfall," so to speak, including the long-awaited Isaac. And God was putting Abraham to the test to see whether he understood all this, or whether he had fallen into the notion that certain things were his by right to possess and keep and preserve as he would.

As you know, Father Abraham passed that test magnificently. By his willingness to give everything back to the One who had given everything to him, he made clear that he did understand the most basic concept of all—that life in all its manifestations is an unmerited gift.

What a difference such a perspective makes when it comes to the practical business of day-by-day living! It frees us from possessiveness and a sense of entitlement; it also enables us to receive the good things in our lives with gratitude and to hold them lightly rather than clutchingly. It even opens the way to relinquishing beloved objects and persons without falling into bitterness and resentment.

In the first sermon I attempted to preach after my daughter's death, I tried to illustrate this vision of life as gift with an experience out of my adolescence. When World War II started, my family was in the habit of sending our clothes to the laundry and so did not own a washing machine. But when gasoline was rationed, my father soon announced that we could not use what little fuel we were allotted to go the several miles to the laundry, and so we faced a genuine domestic crisis.

About that time, a young business associate of my father's was unexpectedly drafted, and we offered to let his family store their furniture in our basement while they were away. It so happened they owned a green Bendix washing machine, and an arrangement was made for us to use the washer in exchange for their using our storage space. Shortly after they left, my mother got sick, and guess who inherited the job of doing the family wash? That meant that for the next three years I developed a very intimate and affectionate relationship with that old machine. I spent many an hour watching the tumbler churn the soapsuds, and I would stick my finger between the rubber roller of the wringer to see how much pressure I could stand.

Then the war ended, and my father's associate returned. One afternoon a trailer came and took all their stuff. I was at school at the time, and when I came home I was shocked to find the basement empty. And I was enraged that the old Bendix was gone. I bounded upstairs angrily and said to my mother, "Somebody has robbed us—the washing machine is gone!"

My mother sat me down then and taught me a lesson that would surface in my mind twenty-five years later. She said, "You have forgotten how the washing machine ever came to be in our basement. It never did belong to us. It always was a gracious gift. That we ever got to use it at all was great good fortune. You relate to gifts differently than you relate to possessions. With gifts, you receive them gratefully, hold them lightly. And when they are taken away, you use that occasion to give thanks that they were ever given at all."

In the depth of my grieving over Laura Lue, it came to me that she was to my life what the old washing machine had been to our family, and that getting to be with her for ten years was infinitely more than I deserved. This realization certainly did not make relinquishing my daughter easy or painless, but it did eliminate my occasion for resentment. It opened the possibility that the God who had given me the good old days could be trusted to give me good new days as well. And this whole perspective came through inter-action with the figure of Abraham and his experience with Isaac. What he remembered on Mount Moriah, we would do well never to forget—that life really is, at bottom, totally gift and grace!

Do you see now why I believe that going back to our biblical forebears can be a rich resource for living more creatively in the present and in the future? Abraham really has been "my father in faith." He has taught me much about life— about the kind of security we can expect with God, about the kind of love God has for us, and most of all, about the kind of reality life is—it is gift, pure and simple in all its manifestations. How helpful it is to be graced with such in-sights!

Questions for Thought and Discussion

1. In what ways is Abraham the Christian's "father of faith"?

2. How does the security God offers differ from what we humans want and have come to expect in our culture?

3. On what does God's love for us and for all humans finally depend?

4. What practical difference does it make to regard every thing you are and have as an entitlement? As an unmerited gift?

5. Can you think of an instance from your own life when you or someone else held on to a person or thing too tightly? Describe the incident.

2

REBEKAH
The Ethics of Obedience

CONTRARY TO WHAT the author of Ecclesiastes thought, things do change. Centuries ago that weary cynic could be heard to sigh, "There is nothing new under the sun," but the inclusion of this chapter in this book effectively refutes that claim.

When I first conceived of writing about our biblical forebears—over fifteen years ago now—it would never have occurred to me to write about our *foremothers* as well as our forefathers. My thinking was a reflection of the conventional thinking of that day; neither I nor society in general had fully understood that sexism is yet another of those "isms"— like provincialism, classism, and racism—that limit us humans in our journey toward wholeness.

However, that situation has changed radically in the last fifteen years. And although there is still much room for improvement, the shift that has occurred both within me and in a large part of our society underlines the reality of newness in the drama of history. Growth and progress clearly move at too slow a pace for many of us, but that does not negate the fact that they do occur and thus offer genuine grounds for hope.

Because my attitude on this subject has changed, this chapter and the subsequent one on Ruth were conceived at a different time than the rest of the material in this book. They represent a "cloud the size of a human's hand" that I hope will continue to grow in the decades ahead. But I must acknowledge my beginner's status in this whole area of thought. Had I waited another five years to work on this project, there would undoubtedly be many more chapters focused on the lives of significant women. For now, however, let this beginning effort stand as the "token" it is and a portent of things to come as all of us learn to appreciate more fully what Jesus saw so clearly nearly two thousand years ago—that the words *male* and *female* are adjectives, not nouns, and that *human being* and *person* are the authentic normative terms.

I have chosen our foremother, Rebekah, for this chapter because I feel her contribution to our religious heritage was absolutely enormous and largely unrecognized or appreciated. She may have had as much to do with keeping the traditions of Abraham alive as any other single person.

To understand her contribution, I believe we must go back to an experience Rebekah's husband, Isaac, had as a young lad—an experience that was destined to leave its mark on him forever.

Even today, the story related in the twenty-second chapter of Genesis is mysterious and awesome—the story of a father willing to sacrifice his own son in obedience to God. Somehow, Abraham became convinced that he was to take Isaac, his long-awaited son of promise, and to sacrifice him back to Yahweh. Was this a carry-over from his days before the gift of the promise, a reappearing of a pagan religious practice? Or, as I suggested in the previous chapter, was it Yahweh's way of finding out whether Abraham really understood the essence of the new way—that life is a gift, that Yahweh could be depended on to provide totally, and that one must never cling idolatrously to any person or possession?

Whatever the nature of Abraham's experience, however, what happened on Mount Moriah must have been absolutely terrifying for the twelve-year-old *Isaac!* Abraham was as noncommunicative at the outset of this journey as he had been when his whole adventure with Yahweh began in Genesis 12. Even Isaac's curious question, "Where is the lamb?" produced no light on what was about to happen. It was not until his father bound him, placed him on the altar, and raised that awful knife that it dawned on Isaac what Abraham was prepared to do, and the whole scene must have frightened the lad out of his wits. To be sure, the hand of Abraham was stayed at the last moment and a ram was finally sacrificed in Isaac's place; but I think it is fair to surmise that the drama on the mountaintop left a permanent mark on the young Isaac.

To state the matter very simply, Isaac proceeded to keep a discreet distance from the God of Abraham all the rest of his days. He did not rebel completely, as other humans have done in response to painful childhood traumas, but neither did he ever venture very close to the One with whom his father had developed so intimate a friendship. Isaac became the kind of adult who preferred more practical and down-to-earth concerns. Years later, when he had twin sons, Isaac gravitated to the one who was a hunter and an outdoorsman by temperament, rather than to the one who was more introspective and religiously inclined. Thus in later years he amplified the choice he had made years before—perhaps as a result of the fright he had experienced. It is never clear just how important any of Abraham's stories about Yahweh and the Lord's promises for the future were to Isaac. The whole tradition might have died of neglect had it not been for the remarkable human being who was drawn onto the stage of God's drama at just this crucial moment. I am referring to our foremother, Rebekah.

Beginning in the twenty-fourth chapter of Genesis, we learn several things about this particular woman who was to become "a saving link" in our salvation story. She was the daughter of a man named Bethuel, who was actually Abraham's nephew, back in the land of Mesopotamia. Like most of the people in that era, the old patriarch was very serious about the issue of racial purity. Thus, when the appropriate time came, he sent his chief servant back to the members of his clan in Ur of the Chaldees to secure a wife for Isaac from among his own kinspeople.

The account of this journey and the part Yahweh played in it is a lovely example of Old Testament "faith-telling." The servant first encountered Rebekah at that great congregating place of ancient culture, the well from which the community literally "drew its life." Rebekah is described here as "very fair to look upon" (24:16, KJV) and quickly proved to be a friendly, hospitable, and unusually helpful human being. She drew water not only for this one, but also for his camels, and before many minutes had passed, a variation on the "love at first sight" theme had transpired. The servant

became convinced that he had found the one for whom he
had made the journey, and he was quick both to give Yahweh
the credit and to begin a process of negotiation with Rebekah's family so that he might secure her to become his young
master's wife.

Was what this one told Rebekah's family her first exposure
to those mysterious stories of Yahweh and the promise that
he had been made to Abraham and his descendants? Perhaps
so. In any event, there was enough intrigue and sense of
positive promise about this visitor and his proposal to prompt
Rebekah to embark on a journey that was every bit as daring
and courageous as Abraham's had been several decades before. Rebekah is pictured as setting out with a stranger to
marry a man she had never even seen, much less met! Here
is the same kind of heroic trust that is always at the heart
of the biblical religion of promise, and it proved to be a
fortuitous event indeed, for the burden of keeping alive those
sacred stories eventually fell to Rebekah's stewardship. Something—perhaps the wounds that went all the way back to
Mount Moriah—had largely weakened Isaac's interest in the
God-dimension of his life. How ingenuous of the Holy One
to call in the likes of a Rebekah for such an hour as this!

The love that developed between Isaac and Rebekah was
a genuine and lifelong reality. In spite of their differences
over the importance of religious concerns and over the twins
that would subsequently be born to them, theirs was an unusually intimate marriage for that era in history, so much
so that the old Book of Common Prayer contained these
words in the service of marriage: "As Isaac and Rebekah
lived faithfully together, so may these persons surely perform
the vows and covenants betwixt them made."

So far in our story, so good. But as the years unfolded,
the same problem that had stymied Abraham and Sarah
emerged for Isaac and Rebekah: they were childless. It is a
measure of how desperate he must have felt to read that
Isaac, of all people, ventured close enough to the awesome
Yahweh to ask for help in this matter! The result was not
simply the gift of conception, but the prospect of twin sons
being born in answer to his prayer. Rebekah, being a creature
of her day, undoubtedly responded to this fact of pregnancy
with both joy and relief. The measure of a female back in

that time was her ability to bear children, especially sons. So for one shining moment Rebekah was ecstatic, because the shame of barrenness had been lifted from her. However, not many months later, she began to experience great turmoil and pain within her womb, and this development disturbed her deeply.

At this juncture, we gain new insight into Rebekah's temperament. Instead of ignoring the trauma within her own body or allowing it to depress her into fearful immobility, she resolved to "inquire of the Lord" about the meaning of the struggle that was taking place inside of her. The answer that she received was a surprising oracle indeed, for it told her something that she would never have known in any other way: "There are two nations in your womb. Your issue will be two rival people. One nation shall have the mastery of the other, and the elder shall serve the younger" (Gen. 25:23, my paraphrase).

Rebekah never forgot that word from Yahweh, and what she heard explains many of the things she did in the future that appear on the surface to be little more than personal preference of one son over the other. Her situation was akin to the one centuries later when a certain Mary was told she would bear a son while still being a virgin. This meant that Mary knew things from God that she was unable to share with anyone else, for who would have believed such an outlandish tale?

In the same way, Rebekah was "let in" on a mystery that defied the customs of that day, which decreed that the first-born male was automatically to be the leader of the clan. As is so often the case, Yahweh's other name here was "Surprise." He intended to strike a blow for gifts, rather than birth order, in determining the role a person assumes in history. And while still bearing these unborn children, Rebekah was given a glimpse of the conflictive drama in which she would be called to participate.

When the day of delivery finally came, Esau emerged first from the womb with Jacob right behind, prophetically holding his brother's foot as if he were tripping him up. The two lads turned out to be radically different in makeup, as we have already noted. Esau was "a hairy man," an outdoorsman and extrovert. Jacob, on the other hand, was a "smooth

man," an introvert and a contemplative sort who stayed close
to the tents of his mother and developed more intellectually
and intuitively than physically.

Not surprisingly, given their early experiences, Isaac was
more drawn to Esau and his enthusiasms, while Rebekah
found it easy to be closer to Jacob and to help him in every
way that she could. I have come to believe that Rebekah
was not simply indulging herself by "playing favorites" with
the child she happened to like the best. John Sanford, in
his book on Jacob entitled *The Man Who Wrestled with God*,
has helped me to see the religious motivations behind Rebekah's actions. The oracle of God that had come to her years
before was her lodestar, and she proceeded to be obedient
to that vision, even though it cost her dearly in terms of
her relationships to other members of her family. Again, as
the mother of Jesus was to learn centuries later, to be "fa-
vored of God" actually means being given a hard task to
perform that may entail great suffering. It does not necessar-
ily confer privileged status or exempt one from difficulty.
Rebekah appears to have taken more seriously than Isaac
how this strange God Yahweh intended to fulfill his promise,
and she proceeded to play her role in this family system
with energy and ingenuity.

For example, Rebekah was the one who overheard Isaac
tell Esau that it was time to pass on the patriarchal blessing,
and she lost no time in seeking to secure this cherished prize
for Jacob. Now, by all common-sense moral standards, what
they did was blatant deception and manipulation and can
only be called indefensible. Yet in light of a larger good—
keeping alive the tradition of Abraham—their actions take
on a very different moral tenor.

The Russian theologian, Nicolas Berdyaev, has noted the
difference between what he calls "the ethics of obedience"
and "the ethics of creativity." The former term refers to
conventional morality, while the latter points to those excep-
tional moments when persons are called to violate lesser
laws in the name of a higher law. What Dietrich Bonhoeffer
did in participating in the plot on Hitler's life and what Martin
Luther King, Jr., did in his acts of civil disobedience during
the 1960s are examples of "the ethics of creativity." John
Sanford suggests that this same process was at work in what

Rebekah and Jacob proceeded to do with the blind Isaac and the insensitive Esau.

There is an old Quaker adage, "The price of purity is irrelevance and the price of relevance is impurity," and this seems to apply to this particular series of events. A tradition that had some validity to it—that the older son should always be the leader of the clan—had become a hardened absolute, and in this case was simply not relevant. In this family, as in many others, giftedness was not a matter of birth order. It was Jacob, not Esau, who had the gifts and inclination to carry on the religious and cultural tradition Abraham had begun. And I find myself applauding our foremother, Rebekah, for her courage and willingness to go against the grain of culture in order to be faithful to a higher law of fulfillment.

Now, it seems clear from the stories that Rebekah was far ahead of her son, Jacob, in terms of personal development. Jacob had wanted power and preeminence over Esau for purely egocentric reasons, and he would later have to go through much painful trauma before his motives were cleansed and purified. However, Rebekah stands out beautifully in these ancient texts as a person who could allow herself to become a means to a higher end. Again and again, we see her breaking out of the stereotypes of her day to do what needed to be done. She sensed a significance to the Abraham stories that wounded Isaac did not see, and she demonstrated a willingness to sacrifice personally in the service of something that was finally bigger than her own life.

The last glimpse that we have of this one in Holy Scripture has her sending Jacob off in haste to her brother, Laban, lest he be killed by a wrathful Esau. As far as we know, Rebekah never saw her beloved Jacob again, and who knows the price she had to pay from Isaac and Esau for the part she had played in deflecting the blessing to Jacob?

Yet Rebekah is numbered in "the glorious company of the sufferers" who know what it means not only to say, but also to act out the principle, "We must obey God rather than men." The fruit of her sacrifice stands out clearly for all of us to see. Can you imagine where any of us in the West would be today if the traditions of Abraham had been entrusted to Esau? These precious insights could well have withered up and died while he was out hunting and fishing.

Jacob was the one created and ordained by God to pass on the saving tradition. Thanks be to Rebekah for the role she played in helping all of this to come to pass as it did. And may the same God empower us all to be as courageous and as perceptive as was our heroic foremother, Rebekah!

Questions for Thought and Discussion

1. Identify the times when Rebekah manifested more courage than the males in that family system. What does that say to our conventional images of masculine and feminine roles?

2. How do you think Esau felt about his mother? Can parents honestly be the same to all their children?

3. What do you think about the concept of "the ethics of creativity"? What are the dangers inherent in it?

4. Can you think of other biblical stories in which the Lord seemed to "strike a blow for gifts, rather than birth order, in determining the role a person assumes in history"? What are they?

5. Have you ever encountered a situation in your own life where you felt you had to make a choice between obeying God and following the prevailing norms of your culture? What did you do?

3

JACOB
Writing Straight with Crooked Lines

JOHN GARDNER, founder of the citizen's lobby Common Cause, once made a very incisive comment on the social turbulence that was rampant in this country in the decade of the 1960s. Every significant institution in our society, he claimed, was caught in a brutal crossfire between "uncritical lovers" and "unloving critics." On the one hand were the utterly naïve who saw nothing at all wrong with our country and responded defensively to any criticism by saying: "America—love it or leave it." At the other extreme were those who were totally negative about our society. "Burn, baby, burn" was their proposal, for only in bringing down every existing structure and starting all over again could the "unloving critics" see any hope for the future.

Gardner was right, I think, in concluding that neither of these extremes was healthy. And when the two collided head-on, as they did in the sixties, no wonder the atmosphere became so heavy and painful for all! Living, growing things—be they a human individual or a corporate reality such as a nation—do not flourish under either absolute approval or wholesale condemnation. What they need, rather, is a proper blending of realism and hope—an unblinking honesty about the present condition of things and also a hope that the present is not all, that there are positive potentials that can grow and develop with appropriate encouragement and facilitation.

Such a blending would amount to what might be called "discerning loving," something very different from the two poles that dominated the sixties. And it is amazing how this very blend of reality and hope is what you find in the pages of the Bible. The biblical writers were neither "uncritical lovers" nor "unloving critics" in the way they depict our spiritual ancestors. There is no slick "Madison Avenue approach" that concentrates only on the positive. But neither is there a dominance of negativism or pessimism or despair. The human beings of the Bible are treated with both honesty and hopefulness. And nowhere is this approach more evident than in the way our ancestor Jacob is depicted.

Here is one of the genuine heroes in the long memory of the Jewish nation, yet no effort is made to gloss over his faults or present him as a wholly admirable or finally perfected character. This one whose story dominates the last half of the book of Genesis is pictured "warts and all"; he was both strong and weak, at times quite trustworthy and at other times deceptive, remarkably courageous and yet also susceptible to cowardliness.

To those of us who find our own experience at times bewildering and ambiguous, such a one seems very close, and great assurance comes when we realize that God is willing to work with the likes of Jacob—warts, weakness, high potential, and all. That is precisely what provides us the energy no longer to evade or deny our own "shadow sides," but to get on with coping and collaborating with God in doing something about them.

There is significance, then, in the form as well as the content of the biblical revelation, and we can be helped by the experience of Jacob precisely because he is not depicted in platitudinous terms.

Make no mistake about it: Jacob really did reflect inconsistencies of behavior right up to the close of his life. For example, in some areas, he was clearly able to learn from experience, modify his behavior accordingly, and become better because of what had happened to him. In other areas, however, he rumbled right on, letting all that had occurred wash over him like water over a closed bottle. Life could be wasted on Jacob, as is clearly evident from his making the same mistakes over and over again.

Let's look first at an area of his life in which Jacob did learn from experience. In the earlier stages of his life, Jacob developed an escapist strategy in dealing with harsh realities.

Again and again he attempted what has been called "a spatial solution" to difficulty—that is, to turn tail and run when anything threatening appeared on the horizon.

This is a strategy we all utilize at the beginning of life, I suppose, but it should not take too long for us to realize that escapism is a solution that really does not solve anything in a practical sense. For one thing, an escapist usually takes the germs of the problem with him or her into the new situation and very quickly reproduces the very same set of circumstances all over again. In addition, when escaping *from* something is one's only concern, that one rarely pays attention to the situation *into which* he or she is fleeing, and the new situation often turns out to be worse than the original one.

The prophet Amos spoke of such a situation as being like fleeing a lion, only to run into a bear (Amos 5:19). This is exactly what Jacob did when he got in trouble with his brother and father at home through manipulation and fled to his uncle in Mesopotamia, only to get in trouble the same way and have to flee again. Jacob—whose name in Hebrew literally means "the trickster"—was forever getting into situations he had to get out of—*fast!*

But something happened to Jacob as he fled from Laban and heard that his brother Esau, whom he had defrauded, was coming to meet him with four hundred armed men. Somehow the escapist grew up, and Jacob stopped running. In that frightening moment, he allowed what he had learned from the past to affect how he acted in the present. He accepted the fact that many times "the only way *out* is the way *through*," that the "good news comes from facing up to the bad news," not running from it. Coming to terms with reality—this is always the first step in dealing creatively with any situation, and all the evidence points to the fact that Jacob internalized these truths and proceeded to adopt a new strategy toward the unpleasant.

To be sure, some of the old manipulative cunning was still a part of Jacob's makeup; he carefully sent his wives and children and several gifts ahead to "soften up" his brother. But it is clear that Jacob intended this time "to face the music," no matter what Esau's reaction was. In this spirit, Jacob spent the night alone by the brook Jabbok, and there found himself wrestling with a manifestation of God Himself. Here was the One with whom Jacob ultimately had to do, the One who never forgets anything and from whom there is no escape. And for all the mystery of this midnight struggle, at least it became evident that Jacob was no longer an escapist; he moved from being an "evader" to being a "facer-upper," and the end result of this was that *he was blessed.*

A new quality emerged in Jacob, echoed in the words, "I will not let you go, unless you bless me"—that is, "until I have learned from this what there is to be learned." And I would suggest that this is a way of coping with difficulty that all of us should emulate. The way out is usually the way through, not around or away. The good news really does come by facing the bad news. Jacob also demonstrated that he was capable of learning from life, of becoming different in the future because of the past. It is possible "to fail forward," as Arthur Gordon once put it, and sad indeed is the person who does not know this and thus allows the experiences of life to be wasted on him or her.

Yet for all the growing that Jacob did in this part of his life, in another area he never did learn, which is why I say he was not consistent or "all together" as we term it today. I am referring now to the way that he treated his sons, showing favoritism to Joseph and Benjamin over the other ten.

The ironic thing about this situation is that Jacob himself had been plagued all his life by the very same problem. He was one of a pair of twins, you will remember, who were born to Isaac and Rebekah. Almost from the start, the parents had divided their devotion—Isaac preferring Esau and Rebekah, Jacob. It must have been a painful thing for a boy in that era of history to be rebuffed by his father, for it was a male-dominated culture. In fact, behind Jacob's cruel deception of his old blind father was undoubtedly a great deal of hostility for what Isaac had done in preferring Esau over him. But even though Jacob had suffered in his own life from this flaw of parental favoritism, when it came his time to be a father, he made the same mistake himself. And he proceeded to work the same kind of havoc among his own children that his father and mother had evoked between him and Esau.

H. G. Wells once observed bitterly that "the only thing

we learn from history is that we do not learn from history." In this important area of his life, this was true of Jacob. And, yet this is what I like about the biblical writers. They were neither "uncritical lovers" nor "unloving critics" in relation to Jacob, or they would not have included both aspects of this genuine paradox in the telling of his story. Jacob never did achieve perfect consistency in his life, but God did not let go of him or abandon him for this reason. How reassuring it is to see in the story of Jacob both the realism and the hope that I need for myself. Do we not all have glaring inconsistencies in our makeups? Who of us can claim to "have it all together"? Yet here is the Good News: *God has not given up on us either!* We are still breathing, which is the most tangible sacrament of hope of which I know, and from this flows the courage to keep on growing.

No attempt is made, then, to gloss over Jacob's inconsistencies, nor are his mistakes swept under the rug or kept out of sight. What happened to Jacob is what happens to all of us—he was most tempted at the points of his greatest strengths, not at the point of his weaknesses. We make a mistake to think too dualistically about good and evil, as if all of one reality is over here and all the other reality is over there. The truth is that good and evil are subtly intertwined, which means that precisely where I can do my best work is also where I am capable of doing the most harm. Any virtue pushed too far can become a vice, and this is vividly illustrated in the story of Jacob.

Unquestionably, Jacob's greatest gift was his drive and ambition and sensitivity to the higher things of life. As a child, he probably sat around the fire and drank in his father's words about the promise that had come to his grandfather Abraham—about how they were no ordinary family, but a people with a great spiritual destiny. Such a heritage must have fired Jacob's idealism to the highest, while his twin brother Esau probably responded in quite the opposite manner.

By temperament, Esau was concerned more for the immediate and the physical than the spiritual. There is no record in all of Genesis of Esau's ever offering a prayer or building an altar or showing any concern for the things of God. And this constituted a problem for Jacob, because at that time the elder son was designated to be the leader of the family in every way—its priest and guide. Since Esau had emerged out of the womb moments before Jacob, he was considered the "firstborn" and therefore the clan leader. What made matters worse was that, as I mentioned in the previous chapter, Isaac was also rather lukewarm about the spiritual side of things. He seemed more interested in the kind of food Esau could hunt and prepare than in his spiritual capabilities, and all this produced great tension in Jacob's spirit.

Realize now it was Jacob's strength, not his weakness, that posed a problem for him at this point. As the story unfolds, Jacob's commendable drive and energy and concern for the things of God led him into some very questionable processes of manipulation and deception that left both Isaac and Esau furious at Jacob and even necessitated his having to flee for his life. I have no doubt that God intended for Jacob to become the spiritual leader of the family, for that was the nature of his giftedness. But as I also mentioned in the previous chapter, his motives and methods at this point were far from mature. Jacob never gave God a chance to work things out in his own way.

The Psalmist speaks of a "zeal" for the Lord's house "eating up" a person (69:9, KJV), and this is the special temptation of the highly committed and the super-dedicated. I repeat: good and evil are not totally separate from each other, but subtly intertwined. Any virtue or strength overdone becomes a vice, which is a warning to all of us to be especially careful in the areas of our greatest giftedness. It is precisely there that our most subtle temptations can be expected to arise.

This is very personal warning to me in relation to the use of words. All my life I have been aware that I had the gift of articulation, but this gift that enables me to bless others can also become a deadly instrument to destroy. This is true across the board; every gift we have been given would make a good present for someone else, but can also be turned into a weapon and become something negative instead of something positive.

One of the deepest meanings of Jacob's struggle by the brook Jabbok lies right at this point. There he had to face up to having run ahead of God and, in his zeal to do right, doing wrong. But having faced this issue squarely, Jacob was given a new name to symbolize his growth. As I have already noted, the name Jacob in Hebrew means "to trick" or "to overreach." By being asked this name by the mysterious Presence, Jacob was forced to acknowledge this tendency in himself. But then he was given a new name: Israel, which in Hebrew means "the one God rules."

This really is the only safe thing to do with our highest potencies—give back to God for instruction what he originally gives to us in creation. We humans are so prone to misuse our gifts, especially our finest powers. The life of Jacob is a healthy warning to us all about the subtle intertwining of good and evil. How fortunate we are that the Biblical writers had never heard of "Madison Avenue" or "public relations" tactics. By seeing how Jacob's best became an occasion for his worst, we are illumined and made aware of the challenge we too must face.

Yet in and around all this honest reporting is the reality of hope that is so crucial. Who can read all the way through the story of Jacob and not see that most glorious truth of all—*that God somehow can write straight with crooked lines.* While it is clear throughout the biblical story that God never wills evil, he is capable of using evil ingeniously to move toward goals of good.

This is seen most clearly toward the end of Jacob's life, years after his favoritism had caused his other sons first to hate Joseph and then to sell him into slavery in Egypt. By all accounts, this was a rotten process, having nothing of goodness or compassion about it. Yet God took that sordid act—"horse manure," if you please—and caused some roses to grow out of it. The descendants of Abraham might have starved to death if a surplus of food had not been accumulated in Egypt. And that surplus might not have been accumulated had it not been for Joseph's presence there. And Joseph might not have been there had it not been for his brothers' hatred and sin. In all Scripture there is perhaps no better example of "writing straight with crooked lines" than in Jacob's story! Joseph himself summed up the whole issue when he said to his brothers, "As for you, you meant evil against me; but God meant it for good" (Gen. 50:20).

That is our final hope, is it not—what God can do with

what we have done to bring order out of chaos and astonishing good out of incredible evil? Second only to creating something out of nothing is this power of his to recycle events, to take what was meant for evil and somehow pick up the pieces and fashion something good out of it all. Jacob and his family survived and lived on because of this amazing capability God possesses. What a source of reassurance that ought to be for all of us in terms of what he might yet bring out of all those things we have brought down by our foolishness.

I am reminded, then, of where this all started—with the Good News that is found not just in the content but in the form of Holy Scripture. The 1960s almost exploded because of the crossfire between "uncritical lovers" and "unloving critics." Neither one of these extremes is good for living things. What we need is a blend of the two—realism and hope, honesty about the way we are, but optimism about what we can become. This is how the biblical writers handle all our forebears, including our father Jacob. Why? Because this is how the God of the Bible handles all people—including us.

Blessed be he!

Questions for Thought and Discussion

1. From which direction—"uncritical lover" or "unloving critic"—do you feel you need to grow toward becoming "a discerning lover"?

2. How do Jacob's obvious inconsistencies make you feel about your own and others' "not-yet-togetherness"?

3. In your own experience, where has a strength gotten you into difficulty or elements of goodness posed specific temptations?

4. What led Jacob to stop running and start facing up to the unpleasant?

5. In what situations in your own life do you tend to apply Jacob's "spatial solution" to difficulty? What kinds of problems do you find it most difficult to face?

4

JOSEPH
How to Fail Forward

GEORGE STEVENSON, a Presbyterian minister who wrote a remarkable book entitled *God in My Unbelief,* tells of a pivotal
experience he had shortly after he had left the seminary and
taken his first church—a small congregation in the Scottish
highlands. Soon after Stevenson began his ministry there,
a crisis erupted in that community. It seems that a tenant
farmer was caught in the act of stealing and was sent to
the local penitentiary. When his sentence was completed, a
local landowner with a sense of social compassion agreed
to give the man a job and to work with him as he attempted
to "turn over a new leaf" and begin again.

However, when the arrangement became known in the
community, an outcry of protest went up. Folk were incensed
at the landowner for bringing a convicted thief back into
their midst, and efforts were made to exclude the convict
and bring pressure on his benefactor.

Stevenson found himself caught squarely in the middle
of this controversy, not only because all the participants were
members of his congregation, but also because he felt the
issue at stake went to the heart of the mission of the church.
As he pondered the dynamics of the situation, Stevenson
realized that what was going on was exactly what Jesus had
predicted at Caesarea Philippi, when he had entrusted "the
keys of the kingdom" to the disciples. Jesus had said: "Whatever you bind on earth shall be bound in heaven, and whatever you loose on earth shall be loosed in heaven." This
meant that what the disciples would do from that time forward would by no means be incidental or peripheral, but

39

would have eternal implications. And this was as true of the
actions in that Scottish church as in the church of the first
century.

You see, Stevenson recognized that the struggle over the
convicted thief was at heart a matter of "binding" and "loosing." Those who wanted nothing to do with the former convict and who resisted all efforts at reclaiming him were in
effect "binding" him to his old ways; their opposition to
his being given another chance only made it that much harder
for him to move in a new direction. The efforts of the compassionate landowner, on the other hand, were aimed at "loosing" the former thief from the past and opening for him
the way into a different kind of future.

What broke the heart of the young minister was the realization that both of these forces were present and at work in
the same church; those who were "binding" and those who
were attempting to "loose" sat side by side every Sunday
morning. Stevenson found himself asking, "How can this
be? How can such divergent approaches emanate from the
same source?" There were undoubtedly many answers to
such a complex question, but Stevenson concluded that the
differences between the "binders" and the "loosers" revolved
around one basic issue: *what these people believed about the possibility of human change.*

I believe this same issue is at the heart of the way we
relate to ourselves and each other today. There seems to
be a growing fatalism on the part of many people concerning
human nature; they seem to have swallowed hook, line, and
sinker the old adage about "the leopard and his spots." Concerning both themselves and other people, they have concluded that the past is the only measure of the future. "Once
a thief, always a thief," they say; "Once an alcoholic, always
an alcoholic. Once a scoundrel, always a scoundrel."

If one really buys into such a conclusion, it is easy to
see how despair and hopelessness can become the prevalent
attitudes toward self and hard-hearted cynicism the dominant
stance toward others. In all likelihood, those folk in George
Stevenson's church who wanted nothing to do with the convicted thief were people who had lost faith in hope. They
no longer believed that a human being could become anything different from what he or she had been, and thus they
scorned all efforts toward change.

Not long ago I ran into a similar expression of rigidity, this time in reference to New Year's resolutions. "They are all a bunch of bunk!" a man said to me. "Hope as a rule makes many a fool. Come January 15, all those high-blown resolves will be long forgotten, and the way it has been will continue to be the way it is forevermore." I am afraid such pessimism characterizes the outlook of a whole host of people these days.

At this point, however, it might be well to ask, "What does the Bible have to say about the possibility of human change?" What we find when we look there is utter realism—coupled with powerful hope. It never speaks of human change as something easy or automatic or painless; the notion of "inevitable progress" has more to do with nineteenth-century romanticism than biblical realism. However, from first to last, it does hold forth the hope that change is possible.

The Bible even goes so far as to say that God is always to be found working on the side of changing people for the good. I dare you to show me a place in all of Holy Scripture where Yahweh comes to a person and commands that one to stay as he or she is! Without exception, the divine invitation is to become something other and better and more than one is at that moment. This was the essence of God's proposal to Abraham and Moses and the children of Israel, and it constituted the first note Jesus struck as he began his ministry in Galilee. He said: "The time is fulfilled, and the kingdom of God is at hand; repent, and believe the gospel" (Mark 1:15). What is this, if not the affirmation that change in human nature is not only possible but highly desirable, and that God is on the side of trying to help this to happen?

The Bible thus calls us to approach all people—ourselves and others—from a stance of hopeful realism or realistic hope. We are not to be naïve and assume that we humans are on some kind of escalator that is automatically lifting us to perfection. People can resist change and even deteriorate from levels once achieved, so there is no room for facile optimism or complacent self-satisfaction. However, the other side of the biblical message is that *change is possible!* People who have acted a certain way for a long time can begin to act in new ways and become something radically different in the future from what they have been in the past. The Bible calls on us not to come to the closure of despair prematurely; we are to be open to the possibility of positive change and to side with whatever efforts are being put forth to bring this about.

A shining example of what I mean by the stance of hopeful realism or realistic hope is found in the stories about our ancestor named Joseph. They comprise the last third of the book of Genesis. As you may remember, Joseph was one of twelve sons born to Jacob, but because he was the first child born of the beloved Rachel, Joseph was immediately singled out as his father's favorite. He proceeded to develop into an arrogant, spoiled child. Everything was given to him and nothing was asked of him, and it is not surprising that by the time he got to be an adolescent he was absolutely insufferable to the whole family. All the other brothers had to work in the field, but Joseph was allowed to lounge around the house in his fabled "coat of many colors," which was literally "a coat with sleeves in it," obviously designed for leisure!

One day his father sent this playboy out into the fields to inquire how his working brothers were doing, and seeing him saunter over the horizon was "the straw that broke the camel's back." Years of pent-up frustration with this whole unfair arrangement erupted, and for a moment it appeared that these angry siblings were going to tear Joseph limb from limb with their own bare hands.

Cooler heads prevailed, however, and as a compromise the brothers sought to rid themselves of Joseph by selling him to some Midianite slave traders. They then took that hated coat, dipped it in blood, and told their father they had found it—that Joseph had obviously been devoured by a wild beast. Needless to say, only brutal and treacherous human beings could have done such a thing to their own brother and father, but such was the measure of their frustration and anger.

The story does not end there, however. The first big surprise is that the pampered Joseph underwent a radical change. Instead of collapsing under this reversal of fortunes, traits in his character that had never been called forth at home began to emerge. When he was sold to an Egyptian army officer, for the first time in his life he was put to work, and qualities of intelligence and efficiency quickly surfaced. Before long, Joseph had risen to the top of all the servants in that household, only to get knocked down again by thwarting Lady Potiphar's advances. He was cast in prison, but not even this injustice daunted his spirit. By faithfully doing the best he could with the opportunities at hand, he eventually came to the attention of the Pharaoh as an interpreter of dreams and was so impressive that the ruler lifted him straight from prison to the number two position of power in all Egypt!

You talk about human beings undergoing change! This story makes the modern legends of "rags to riches" and "log cabin to White House" seem pale by comparison! Who would have predicted, given that pampered "hothouse plant" back in Palestine, that this kind of human being would emerge? But that is just the point. Joseph's story shows that change *is* possible, even for the most unlikely people, even though it is by no means inevitable.

Several years after Joseph's meteoric rise to power, a famine he had predicted swept over the whole Fertile Crescent, and Joseph's brothers came to Egypt in search of food. Joseph recognized these kinsmen of his, but quite understandably they never suspected his identity. It would have been a perfect occasion to settle an old score. Now that Joseph had the upper hand, what could have been more gratifying than giving these brutal men a dose of their own medicine?

However, this was not at all what Joseph set out to do. Tempered, perhaps, by his own experience of change, he was intent on finding out if what had happened to him across the years had also happened to his brothers. Had they too become different persons because of what they had experienced?

This question, I believe, was behind all the strange things Joseph began to do to his unsuspecting brothers. When I first read these accounts, I wondered about this business of putting money in the food sacks, demanding that Benjamin come down the next time, and then arranging things so that this other "favorite son" of Rachel would be detained and enslaved. It all seemed so senseless and cruel, until I realized that Joseph was testing his brothers. You see, he believed that change was possible, but he knew it was not inevitable or automatic. All these maneuvers were his way of seeing if anything had altered across the years.

And lo and behold, it turned out that Joseph was not the

only person in his family who had undergone transformation!
It soon became clear that these persons who had once lashed
out at their father for his favoritism now had a new kind of
concern for him, and instead of treating Benjamin the way
they had once treated Joseph, they treated him with tender
protectiveness. It literally brought tears to Joseph's eyes to
see Judah step forth and offer to go into slavery himself
rather than see Benjamin detained. Here was a one-hundred-
and-eighty-degree shift! The same brother who years before
had sold his own flesh and blood into slavery was now willing
to accept slavery himself rather than to hurt his father again.

This then is the biblical answer to the question: "Can human nature change?" Is the leopard and his spots a valid
analogy for human beings, or can we become something very
different from what we were in the past? The Bible clearly
says no to the first question and yes to the second. Change
in human behavior *is* possible—not inevitable or painless
or easy, but infinitely possible—and this is the stance of hopeful realism or realistic hope that we are called to assume in
the world.

Joseph had every right to prove his brothers and not naïvely
assume that the passing of years had automatically perfected
them. By the same token, to have concluded ahead of time
that they were the same as he had once known them would
have been to have missed the great thing that occurred. It
does not pay to underestimate the forces in personality that
are resistant to change, for there are many, but neither should
we underestimate the power of new expectations, the work
of an active conscience, the power of seeing the consequences
of our misdeeds played out on the lives of others. Joseph
became something different in a new setting because something different was asked of him. And the workings of conscience and the grief of an old man served to turn once
unfeeling brothers into genuinely different human beings.

That is the kind of change that is possible in our world,
and the story of Joseph reminds us of this truth in powerful
ways. Like those folk in that Scottish village, we are constantly
in the process of "binding" or "loosing" both ourselves and
other people; we are making it harder or easier for folk to
become "less of what they used to be and more of what
they ought to be." And chances are, the whole process turns

on this one issue: what do we believe about change? Do we think it is possible for a human being to become different?

If somewhere back up the line we have come to a negative conclusion at this point, both despair and rigidity will surely set in. Those folk who opposed a thief being given another chance must have honestly felt this way. However, the Bible does not support such a position. It is by no means naïve in this regard, as if change for the good were automatic or easy. But the Bible is hopeful—realistically hopeful that one can "fail forward," that is, learn from mistakes and fashion a future that is genuinely different from the past. I believe the Bible calls the church to follow the example of that compassionate landowner rather than the fearful protestors. The God of the Bible is always to be found on the side of hope, trying to fan whatever flicker of promise he can toward a new future. This One is forever meeting us as he met Abraham of old—with a vision of a better tomorrow. Can we call ourselves followers of such a One and do anything less?

Questions for Thought and Discussions

1. Do the images of "binding" and "loosing" make more sense to you now because of the drama in the Scottish village? In which stance do you feel you have mostly been up to now?

2. What factors in Joseph's life made him what he was at home and then in Egypt?

3. Why do you think Joseph recognized his brothers and they failed to recognize him? Do expectations color our interpretations of the present?

4. What are some of the factors that make genuine human change so difficult? In other words, why is it so hard for us to make changes in their lives—even when the change is for our benefit?

5. At what points in your life do you now sense "God writes straight with crooked lines?"

5

MOSES
Secrets of Growing with God

MEMORY IS a crucial component of identity. If we would come to terms with who we are and what we can be, we must take into account what we have been and all that vast and ambiguous background out of which we have come. This is true in every way, which is why the Old Testament is so important in our religious unfolding. It tells of that deep root-system from which we Christians grow, and learning both about and from some of these pivotal individuals is a way of living deeper and deeper into the mystery of our own reality.

Our focus now is on one of the most towering figures in the Bible. I am referring specifically to Moses, the legendary deliverer and lawgiver who served as midwife in the birth of the nation Israel. There are other characters who loom as large in the pages of the Old Testament, but none had any greater practical impact on the shaping of our heritage than this one. What was the secret of his life, and how was he able to do all that he did? The material is far too voluminous to cover exhaustively in only one chapter. Therefore, let us focus in on just two areas—his relation to God and his relation to the Hebrew people—to see if we can discover in these areas clues both to the genius of Moses and to our own human potential.

Obviously, Moses' interaction with this God called Yahweh was the central experience of his whole life. He was a descendent of Abraham and Sarah, you will recall, but by this time this family had migrated down to Egypt and become enslaved by the Pharaoh there. It was from his Hebrew parents that

Moses undoubtedly heard the traditions about this God Yah-weh who had acted so decisively in history and who had chosen the Hebrew people for a purpose. Such a vision must have taken deep root in Moses' mind, for even though he individually was lifted out of the plight of his people through being adopted by the Pharaoh's daughter, he never forgot this image of a God who is active in history and specifically concerned about the Hebrews.

Moses began, then, with a general idea about the Holy One. But as his story unfolds, it becomes clear that he had much to learn about how this God actually works in the day-by-day experiences of life. Like all adolescents, who are given to the grandiose and the dramatic, Moses started out expect-ing the spectacular. This sort of thinking undoubtedly lay behind his brash act of killing the Egyptian slave master who was abusing a Hebrew. I am confident the young idealist thought a revolution would begin at that moment—that God would reach down from heaven to cut the Gordian knot of enslavement in one grand gesture, that the Hebrews would rise up as one person and seize their freedom.

Imagine, then, Moses' great dismay when nothing immedi-ately happened in response to his violent act. God did not send lightning from heaven, and the Hebrews began to mur-mur distrustfully rather than rallying to him. And when word got to the Egyptians of what Moses had done, he had to flee for his life into the desert, his grandiose dream of libera-tion in shambles.

This was a crucial rite of passage for Moses—the point at which his childhood dreams and fantasies collided rudely with reality. Many people never negotiate this stage of devel-opment; they either revert to childlike illusion and live forever in pathetic fantasy or give up altogether and become cynical and closed off. Significantly enough, like the prodigal son in Jesus' parable, Moses chose to make neither of these re-sponses. Instead, he proceeded to "come to himself," and grow up—to relinquish both fantasy and despair and go on about the business of living in the real world.

At this point, perhaps the traditions of family lore helped Moses to grow as he did, for there alone in the desert he may have remembered how one of his ancestors, a man named Joseph, had handled a similar experience. Joseph, too, had begun the pilgrimage of personhood with a grandiose image of himself and God, and by acting impatiently and arrogantly had caused himself to be rejected by his kins-people. And Joseph had also become a lonely refugee far from home. But Joseph had not given up in the face of such adversity. Instead, he had stopped dreaming all those grandi-ose things about himself and his destiny and had gone to work on the situation at hand.

This had been the crucial breakthrough for Joseph—learn-ing to be attentive and faithful to the realities within his reach. And it had been in day-to-day struggles that Joseph had discovered God to be at work. He is not just the Lord of the spectacular; he is to be found in little things as well, and this is how God had worked in the life of Joseph. He had become Grand Vizier of Egypt not by storming the gates, but by patiently and faithfully handling little details—first as a slave, then as a prisoner. The "mill of God" had ground slowly for Joseph and involved much struggle. I am guessing such a memory was of enormous help to Moses when, "fresh out of prep school" and ready to conquer the world, he found himself a total failure, wandering the wastes of the Sinai desert.

Like Joseph before him, Moses did not give up or collapse, but his vision of God began to change. He started to see Yahweh not only as a God who works through miracles and thunderbolts, but also as One who works with us in the day-to-day struggle with little things. And so Moses settled down to make not just the best, but the most, of the opportunities that were at hand. He became a shepherd in that desert region and proceeded to learn the terrain of a country that he would one day need to know in leading a whole people. More impor-tantly, he learned to be patient with a God "whose ways are not as our ways and whose thoughts are not as our thoughts"—One who is always good but not always obvious.

It was this attentiveness to detail, this willingness to let God be who he was and do what he would do, that led up to Moses' call forty years later. On the back side of the Sinai desert one day, he noticed a phenomenon he could not ex-plain—a bush was on fire but was not burning up. Had he regressed or become cynical about life, he would never have noticed such a seemingly insignificant happening. But that was just the point—Moses had stopped looking for God only in the overwhelming and had learned to be sensitive to the so-called "little things." The text says Moses turned aside to explore more fully this thing he could not explain (Exod. 3:3). And there he encountered Yahweh and was commissioned to do on the Lord's terms what years before he had attempted on his own. This is how the great work of liberation was begun—not with some cataclysmic sign in the sky, but with a single bush burning on the back side of the desert.

This is such an important point to learn, I think, about our human interaction with God. There are moments of miracle and ecstacy when God for his own purpose breaks in from beyond and intervenes in the ordinary flow of things. He did some of that in the course of finally getting the Hebrews out of Egypt—there were the plagues and the parting of the water and the manna and the quail. But far more common than such extravaganzas is the quiet collaboration in day-to-day struggles and the ability given to endure long stretches when nothing seemed to be happening. We run a real danger of setting people up for disillusionment if we imply that "Miracle is God's only name." At times, to be sure, he does enter history in this form, but it is by no means the only way.

The growth that we see in Moses' understanding of what ńe could expect of God can be helpful indeed to all of us in knowing what *we* can expect. More often than not, God does things with us and not for us, and sometimes only gives us the strength to endure circumstances rather than to change them. And so often it is we ourselves—not the conditions around us—that do the changing.

Such a widened understanding of how God works is what I believe sustained Moses throughout his long struggles, and it has to be one of the reasons he was able to accomplish as much as he did. He was not finally disappointed, because his Hebrew kinspeople did eventually get out of Egypt into the land of promise. Moses' perceptions of Yahweh grew, and we would do well to grow with him. Disillusionment is almost always the child of illusion. To expect wrongly is to be disappointed. Moses' growth in God can be a powerful corrective to this happening to us.

A second clue into the power of this man lies in his attitudes and actions toward the people he was called to help. And I believe we can learn a lot from him when it comes to helping other people grow and mature—whether it is our own children, those who work under us, or the underdeveloped segments of our society and our world.

First of all, Moses was willing to get involved, to cast his lot with his Hebrew kinspeople. Remember, although he was a Hebrew by birth, he had been adopted by Pharaoh's daughter and raised in the palace as an Egyptian prince. By virtue of these opportunities, he had become quite different from his relatives who were languishing in slavery. How easy it would have been for him to have turned his back on his people and contented himself with privilege!

I really believe there are just two kinds of folk: those who work to make the world a better place for everyone and those who work to make a better place for themselves in the world as it is. Moses was of the former stripe. He could have taken for granted the enormous good fortune that had befallen him and forgotten all about his downtrodden kinspersons, *but he did not!* What was happening to them made a difference to him. He could not rest in luxury while they were languishing under oppression, and so he chose the way of true morality: he voluntarily took on problems he could have avoided on behalf of his brothers and sisters. And let it be said that this is the only way progress can be made in the area of social justice—when those who are not involved as victims are willing to become involved on behalf of victims.

But that is actually only one side of the matter, and Moses was quick to learn the other side, which is that maturing and liberating can only be done *with* and not *for* other people. His act of killing the Egyptian overlord was an honest attempt to hand his people freedom on a silver platter, but freedom does not work that way. Like maturity or education or anything of a personal nature, freedom must be claimed and participated in by the people themselves. You do not inject realities like this into people like penicillin. The victims must want to be different and be willing to participate in their own "healing" before any significant change can occur.

This is why the more mature Moses came back from the desert and spoke first to the Hebrews before he did any confronting of Pharaoh. He needed to know whether they wanted to be free and, if so, whether they were willing to

take and pay for that human treasure. And this time he found
that they were ready. This participatory willingness on the
part of the Hebrews was as much an ingredient in the Exodus
event as Moses' willingness to forgo ease and get involved
with them.

There were other significant aspects of Moses' relation
to these people. One was that he realized the movement
from slavery to freedom could not be simple or instant. For
people who had had no freedom for four hundred years,
who had been totally regimented in every aspect of their
lives, it was an enormous leap suddenly to be on their own,
and it is no wonder that the Hebrews floundered and fumbled
a great deal at first. Who of us does anything perfectly the
first time around? Moses understood this basic fact and was
therefore patient and affirming, as one has to be in order
to facilitate maturity.

Moses also knew that responsibility must develop through
the exercise of freedom; it cannot be a prerequisite for freedom. The Exodus account makes it very clear that the Hebrews were unprepared for the responsibilities of self-
determination in the desert, but giving them freedom was
the only means to that end. How can someone learn to be
responsible until he or she is given something for which to
be responsible? What a cruel mistake it would be to say to
a child, "I will give you a book after you learn to read, or
let you go in the water after you learn to swim." The only
way we learn to handle anything responsibly is through actual
participation. I believe we have much to learn in this area
when it comes to teaching our children and relating to the
underdeveloped classes in our society. We have tended to
place freedom at the end rather than the beginning of the
maturing process, and this never works. There will be mistakes and failures and genuine suffering, to be sure, but how
else does responsibility grow?

Overarching all of Moses' relations to the nation of Israel,
however, was an incredible love that "bore all things, believed
all things, hoped all things, endured all things" (see 1 Cor.
13). His identification with them and sacrifice for them would
have been "sounding brass and tinkling cymbal" had it not
been for the profound affection he had for these people.
Moses' finest hour came when he descended from Sinai, the

Law in hand, to find these childlike former slaves worshiping a golden calf. As you know, his first reaction was to throw down the tablets in rage and vent his profound frustrations at having to deal with such a difficult people. What parent has not had such moments of utter fury and frustration with the task of maturing another human being? Yet when the anger and frustration subsided, there beneath it was a love that would not go away. So we see Moses wearily climbing up the mountain again to intercede for these same folk! He even offered for God to blot him out if necessary rather than give up on these children.

I sometimes wonder in relation to our own children, and in relation to the poor and underdeveloped in our own country and in the world, whether we have Moses' spirit and undying sense of love? If *we* do not—those of us who by good fortune are the privileged of the earth—maturity can hardly be expected to come to them, and if it does not, woe unto the rest of us! The book of Exodus is a classic manual of what is involved in helping a people who were "no people" develop into responsible persons, and as parents and citizens of this world we would do well to look there and learn before it is too late. Moses knew how to facilitate maturity. Is there a more needed human skill just now in our world?

Which brings me back to where this chapter started—this towering figure of a man who more than any other left his mark on Old Testament religion. What was the secret of Moses' greatness? How did he do what he did? I certainly do not have all the answers, but a place to begin would have to be with his special understanding of the way God works and his unparalleled ability to love his kinfolks into maturity. What a legacy that continues to be for us!

Questions for Thought and Discussion

1. With what attitude did Moses regard the things that happened to him in history?

2. How does Moses' earlier view of God correspond to your childhood and adolescent perceptions?

3. Can you identify some of the sources of Moses' patience and hope during his exile in the desert?

4. What were some times in your life when you longed to do something "significant" but could only be faithful in taking care of the little details of your life? In retrospect, what can you say about those times?

5. What can Moses teach us today about the tasks of parenting and social development?

6

SAMSON
The Failure of Promise

WHENEVER THE SUBJECT of family trees comes up, someone usually trots out the old saw about not wanting to look very far for fear of finding some of his ancestors hanging from one of the limbs. Such a remark is actually an acknowledgment of what is true of every one of us—that there are some "bad apples" in all of our personal backgrounds. This is the case with every family I know, and it is also true of the spiritual ancestry that is traced for us in the Old Testament. I have already noted with gratitude that the biblical writers make no attempt to whitewash the lives of our forebears. Neither Abraham nor Rebekah nor Jacob nor Moses was by any means perfect; they were all very much mixed creatures like ourselves. However, in these four cases the balance of strengths and weaknesses did come out on the positive side.

Unfortunately, that is more than I can say for the man we come to consider now. While we do not exactly find him "hanging from one of the limbs" of our spiritual family tree like a horse thief, his story is nonetheless one of tragedy and failure. Yet I believe even this can be instructive to us if we will allow it.

I am referring, of course, to that hero-judge of Israel named Samson. When I use the terms *tragedy* and *failure* to describe his life, I do not mean to take anything away from his attractiveness or appeal as a human being. In this regard, Samson had all the gifts that any human being could have possessed— strength, daring, flash, likeability—and his exploits were the kind that make for great drama and entertainment. The four chapters in Judges that chronicle his life (13–16) are masterpieces of storytelling, and I imagine that around the fire at night the stories about Samson regaled not only the children but also the partisan Hebrews who liked to hear how one of "their boys" had outsmarted and gotten the best of an enemy.

For example, one time the people with whom the Hebrews had the most trouble—the Philistines—had given Samson a raw deal, and he proceeded to "show them." He went out and singlehandedly caught three hundred wild foxes, tied them in pairs, put flaming torches in their tails and turned them loose in the Philistine's grain fields. As someone has irreverently commented, this is the first reference in history to "taillights," and the Hebrews must have held their sides at the thought of such a sight. Or then there was the time that Samson was down in Gaza and the Philistines locked the gates of the city one night to trap him. Samson responded by uprooting the gates, posts and all, carrying them twenty miles, and depositing them on a hillside.

As far as providing delightful material for storytelling goes, Samson ranks right along with Hercules or Paul Bunyan or any other of the legendary heroes. But the tragedy I referred to lies at a deeper, more serious level. It is not just what Samson was, but what he was meant to be and could have been, that casts a shadow across this story. Samson was magnificently endowed by God to be a great leader of his people in a time of need. The children of Israel had entered the Promised Land by this time and were hard at the task of trying to establish themselves in a new environment. Samson was to have been instrumental in this process, yet he never lived up to his extraordinary potential. He spent his days, rather, as something of a buffoon and as an ineffectual playboy.

The question needs to be asked: "Why was this so? How did one who had all the makings of a winner wind up at the end such a loser?" In order to answer this question, I want us to look at Samson's family background, for here perhaps are some clues to the kind of person he chose to become.

The home into which Samson was born was an unusually devout one. His parents had been childless for years when one day an angel appeared to Samson's mother and announced that she would conceive and bear a son. In response to such a promise, the woman took what is called "a Nazarite vow," which symbolized absolute dedication unto God. As an outward sign of such a commitment, the person agreed to abstain from all wine and strong drink and any ceremonially unclean food, and also not to let a man-made razor touch the hair that God had given. This was a special asceticism, comparable to entering a monastery in our day, and it was taken either for life or in preparation for a special task. The fact that Samson's mother took such a vow not only for herself but for the promised child as well denotes the deep religious piety that characterized Samson's home.

His father, a man named Manoah, was no less earnest. When he heard what had been announced to his wife, he was just as excited as she and proceeded to offer one of the finest parental prayers to be found in all Scripture. He said: "O my Lord, let the man of God whom thou didst send come again unto us, and teach us what we shall do with the child that shall be born" (Judg. 13:8, RSV). This is exactly how anyone should react to the awesome news that he or she is about to be entrusted with a human life—asking God to send along with the child the accompanying wisdom to discharge the task. Here again is evidence of a piety that is striking indeed.

However, over against this genuine intensity there was not, at least on the part of the father, a balancing quality of insight. Manoah felt more deeply than he thought. I base this conclusion on the way he reacted when his prayer was answered and an angel did come to instruct these two about rearing the child. Manoah entertained this one and together the couple made an offering to God, and then the angel disappeared upward in the flame of the altar.

Only at this point did it dawn on Manoah that they had been visited by a messenger of God. At that he cried out in terror, "We will surely die, for we have seen God."

This was an age-old idea, rooted in pagan distrust, that the consequence of meeting with a god was instant annihilation. Manoah made no attempt to think out the events that had just occurred. He rather reverted to the superstitions of his childhood and dissolved in panic. It was his wife who had to put things together for him. She said: "Wait a minute, Manoah. *Think!* If God were going to kill us, would he have accepted our offering? Would he have come to us with this promise or instructed us in what to do? Don't you realize the implications of what has happened? We have been given a promise. Will God destroy what he has just proposed to begin?"

Manoah is a classic example, it seems to me, of a kind of piety that is uninformed by thought, of a religion that lurches from emotion to emotion without ever trying to think out the ways of God with humankind. Now to be sure, there is always mystery and paradox at the heart of true religion; we can never know God perfectly or get all reality to fit neatly in an airtight system. But that does not mean that we should not try to make as much sense as possible out of what is happening to us religiously. I believe that our minds are as much a gift of God as our emotions and that the command to think is just as valid religiously as the command to feel. It is not enough just to be zealous or passionately committed. The need for careful thought is just as great as the need for emotional intensity, and this condition in Samson's background may furnish a clue as to why he developed as he did in adulthood.

It is entirely possible that Samson spent his whole life reacting against the emotional fanaticism of his parents. As we just noted, they were committed, devout people and lived what we would call a narrow, rigid life. No attempt was made, perhaps, to show Samson why certain things were done or to explain the reason behind particular practices. As was true of the Puritans of a later date, religion in Samson's home may have become a matter of rigid authority and blind negativism; if this is the case, he would not have been the first to rebel against such rigidity and go to the other extreme.

There is much about Samson's behavior to support this possibility, for he was never remotely serious about the things that were important to his parents. He was forever a playboy—sensuous, impulsive, erratic; he developed none of those characteristics seen in that devout mother taking her vow or that serious father asking for guidance. By being too rigid, too negative, too authoritative, and by never thinking through with the boy why all their pious activities were carried out, Samson's parents may have set the stage for an adolescent rebellion out of which Samson never chose to grow.

However, one could just as easily argue the other way and say that Samson's adult life was not a reaction to, but a repetition of his father's qualities. If Manoah had trouble thinking things through or putting things together in a coherent way, so did Samson. In fact, you might say this was at the root of many of his problems throughout his adult life. One definition of maturity suggests that one moves from seeing life as a jumble of isolated particulars to being able to see patterns and to organize these particular parts into some configuration of meaning. This is something the adult Samson was never able to do. There is little evidence of such coherence in the way he dealt with his own emotions, in the way he went about understanding himself, or in the way he treated other people.

For example, Samson never got beyond the level of acting out what he was feeling at a given moment. There was no such thing as "delayed gratification" in Samson's experience. Whatever he felt like doing at the time—good or bad—is what he did, which meant that no one could count on him or have any basis of ongoing relationships with him.

Samson also failed totally to come to terms with himself and to discover that secret of identity that held together the many diverse parts of his being. Perhaps the best-known episode of Samson's life was his encounter with the Philistine woman Delilah, and it dramatizes what can happen when one never goes to the trouble to do his or her "homework" and thus is oblivious to one's particular uniqueness.

By this time, Samson had become something of a legend to the Philistines because of his destructive behavior, and when they found out he was infatuated with one of their women, they offered her a fantastic bribe to uncover the secret of his strength and capture him. Now obviously, Samson had never approached the question of his identity in reflective terms; he had never bothered to inquire much into this question of who he was. He did know his mother's story about the Nazarite vow and that he was never to cut his hair, but he did not value that part of his life or understand its relation to the other aspects of his being. Samson lived what Socrates would later call "the unexamined life," and thus was tragically vulnerable to a real attack on his being.

When Delilah first asked Samson about the secret of his strength, overgrown child that he was, he responded playfully. He was so unaccustomed to serious self-reflection that he did not even realize what she was doing or what her intentions were. But at last she got to him. With the age-old weapon of a woman's tears, Delilah got Samson to tell her the secret about his hair, and with that she promptly lulled him to sleep, cut it off, and separated him from his potency.

"Give your life away, but do not throw it away," a wise man once said to me. But how can one do this if one has never come to term with one's own secret? Samson had not, and this, of course, was his undoing. He threw his secret away to one who did not really care for him, and she used it against him. The Philistines came and easily captured him, put out his eyes, and reduced him to an object of sport and ridicule.

As I read this account, I thought how tragic it was that Samson had not been moved to discover his secret by someone who loved him. After all, the world is full of Delilahs, people who want to know our secrets solely to manipulate us. For example, there is a whole field of industrial psychology intent on finding out all it can about the human secret so that they can sell us something and use us in ways that further their ends. Like it or not, we live in a world that will exploit our secret if it can, which makes it all the more imperative that we learn to love ourselves properly so that we can avoid "throwing away our lives." Samson was never serious about putting together a coherent sense of self out of which to do business with the world, and this fact more than any other accounts for the failure of this one who possessed such extraordinary natural gifts.

I could go on to point out other areas where Samson never thought things out or put all the particulars of life together, but suffice it to say that one who started out with such great promise to bless ended his life in a flurry of destruction. The Philistines had put out both his eyes and made him do the work of an animal amid their taunts and jeers. Finally one day they brought him out at one of their cultic gatherings. After he had been paraded around in ridicule, he asked to be taken to the place where the pillars that held up the roof were located. There he prayed one last prayer—a petition of anger and hostility and revenge: "Please, God, restore my strength one more time, that I may give these dogs a taste of their own medicine" (my paraphrase).

What a contrast to Jesus' last prayer: "Father, forgive them; for they know not what they do." But you see, what Jesus had done—put together all his life, even his enemies, into a coherent whole—Samson had never done. All he managed to do in the final act of his life was to kill himself and in the process to take more Philistines down with him than he had ever killed before.

What a waste! What a tragedy! But thus ended the saga of Samson. He could have given his life away so effectively for the Hebrew people, but he chose instead to throw it away. To be sure, there were some shadows in his family background that may have influenced him to live as he did, but in the final analysis what he did with his life was his own fault—not his mother's or father's.

That leaves us with a question: Will we learn anything from Samson's example? His story is a warning to us to think through our lives—particularly this question about our secret, the source of our strength, that good thing God had in mind when he created each of us. We have the responsibility to discover this secret, accept it, and give it away creatively. If we do not, if we ignore it, we may—like Samson—end up throwing it away.

Questions for Thought and Discussion

1. What do you think were the major flaws in Samson's personality?

2. How did Samson's early home life compare with your experiences in growing up?

3. Have you known individuals who, like Manoah, failed to balance their passionate commitment with a measure of thought and insight? What about those who erred in the other direction—who gave a great amount of thought and discussion to an issue without ever committing themselves to action? Which of these is your primary tendency?

5. Have you encountered many people like Delilah whose interest in you is basically manipulative? Identify them and explore how best to relate to them.

7

RUTH

The Wisdom to Make Your Move

AUTHOR SAM KEENE once defined a wise person as "one who knows what time it is in his or her life," that is, one who senses what is appropriate to do in a given situation. Such a quality is to be highly prized indeed, for hardly an hour goes by in our human pilgrimage without the need to make some decision. More often than not, this decision boils down to the question: "Should I accept these conditions that I face and proceed to learn to make the best of them, or am I facing a challenge to alter these circumstances and change the conditions?"

The life of the ancestor we come now to consider furnishes a beautiful commentary on this question and on the whole subject of wisdom. I am referring now to our foremother Ruth and to that lovely Book in the Old Testament that bears her name. Here is one of the finest examples of Hebrew storytelling in all Holy Scripture. The term *idyll* could rightly be applied to these four chapters, for there is not a single villain or reprehensible act recorded in these pages. With just the right amount of detail, some ancient author has given us a glimpse of one of our forebears who is well worth our understanding and even emulating.

The issue of when to acquiesce and when to fight back meets us in the very first lines of the Book of Ruth. It seems that a famine developed in the southern part of Israel and forced a real crisis of decision for a certain Elimelech and his family. Tradition has it that he was a potter by vocation. There was so little money around his home village of Bethlehem that the issue of sheer survival began to press in more and more dramatically. Rather than simply give up in resignation, Elimelech did what many of his forebears all the way back to Abraham had done; he exercised the courage to venture into a foreign land in hopes of finding more resources. He and his wife, Naomi, and their two sons went east to the land of Moab and there established a more suitable basis for their lives.

The people who lived in Moab were distant kinspersons of the Hebrews. They were the descendants of Lot, a nephew of Abraham who had started with that patriarch on his great venture of promise centuries before. This was also the land through which the Israelites had moved before crossing the Jordan River into Palestine—the land of Mount Nebo, where Moses had looked over into "the land of milk and honey" just before he died and was buried. In Elimelech's bold move to seek a livelihood rather than to starve slowly, one sees the quality of wisdom being lived out.

But then tragedy struck again, for Elimelech died and left Naomi and her two sons in the land of Moab. If the tradition be true that the sons were also potters, then once again the family faced a moment of crisis and demonstrated real courage and appropriate discernment by deciding to stay with their business and establish themselves in Moab not as outsiders but as a real part of the Moabite culture. This is what Naomi's arranging for her sons to marry two Moabite girls meant. Since the Moabites were of a different racial heritage, this decision represents a far-sighted willingness to rise above the conventions of that day.

The late Carlyle Marney used to say that one of the great challenges of our human venture is "getting the adjectives and nouns of life in their proper places." An adjective, according to Marney, points to some important characteristic about a human being but never tells the whole story. For example, the words *tall* and *short* are adjectives. Each says something very significant about the shape of a human body, but neither of these words say everything there is to be said about the mystery of a person. *Human being* or *child of God* are the definitive nouns; all other words simply point to one facet of a given human being.

However, the history of our planet is replete with the tragedy of adjectives getting elevated to the place of nouns; that is, one aspect of a person becomes regarded as the only thing of significance about that person. Who of us who were raised in the southern part of the United States can fail to realize that the adjective *Negro* used as a noun carried with it the implication that nothing mattered about the person except his or her race? Similarly, the words *male* and *female* have also been used to define rather than describe human beings.

There is perhaps no clearer way of describing Christian redemption than to say that Jesus effectively got the nouns and adjectives of life in their proper places. Looking back on the impact of his ministry, St. Paul could say with good reason, "There is neither Jew nor Greek, there is neither bond nor free, there is neither male nor female . . . in Christ Jesus" (Gal. 3:28, KJV). Jesus took the vast diversity of the human family and arranged those differences horizontally rather than vertically. This means that he took seriously the particulars about each individual he encountered and let these adjectives have their proper significance. But he never took these partial modifiers and made some kind of hierarchical system of them so that one characteristic puts a person "up" while another puts that one "down."

There was a marvelous sense of equality in the way Jesus interacted with all the diversity that he encountered, and in the life of our ancestor Ruth we see a glimmer of this same kind of inclusive wisdom. The words *Hebrew* and *Moabite* were regarded as adjectives by Naomi and her sons. The fact that Orpah and Ruth had a different racial background was considered seriously, but not of ultimate importance and I find myself applauding all five of these human beings for their willingness to reach beyond the conventional prejudices of that day and do something that was most appropriate to the realities of their situation.

I believe the decision Naomi and her family made is in line with the whole thrust of biblical religion. We need to remind ourselves constantly that too much isolation makes for sterility, and that the secret of creativity lies in bringing together those things that are different and allowing their interaction to give birth to the new.

Think about it for a moment. Human procreation, for example, occurs when two human beings who are significantly different from each other come together in intimacy and out of their diversity bring forth new life. The only way any of us ever learns anything is by getting close enough to someone who knows things we do not know that our knowledge can thus be enlarged.

Centuries after Ruth died, one of her descendants would select for his inner circle of disciples a tax collector named Matthew and a member of the Zealot Party named Simon. You could not find two human beings more different in temperament or commitment than these two. Yet Jesus sensed that each of them had value and that in a profound way each needed the creative corrective that interaction with the other would afford. It was consistent with his teaching that our fulfillment often lies in loving our enemies and venturing close to the "not-like-ourselves."

When Jesus asked, "If you love [only] those who love you, what reward have you?" (Matt. 5:46), I think he was referring to the fact that diversity is the source of creativity. We experience enrichment and enlargement through interaction with those other than ourselves. Therefore, when Naomi and her sons not only decided to stay in Moab after Elimelech's death, but also to enter more fully into the culture through intermarriage, we see this quality of courageous wisdom being acted out. And in the process we also see a significant foremother of our religious heritage being invited onto the stage of biblical history.

After Naomi and her sons made the decision to settle in Moab, tragedy struck this family system a second blow. Both of the sons, Mahlon and Chilion, died as their father before them and another crisis was precipitated. Now there were three widows left to fend for themselves.

To understand the seriousness of this situation, we need to remember that the culture of that day was totally dominated by males. A woman was considered both the property and responsibility of some male, which meant that any female who did not have a father or a husband or a brother or a son to take care of her was in desperate straits. There were really only two alternatives open to such a woman—to sell herself into slavery or to resort to prostitution.

It was difficult, indeed, for Naomi to decide what to do. But once again, this quality of wisdom—"knowing what time it was in her life"—becomes manifest in her life. Word had reached her by means of the caravans that traveled through that the famine back in Bethlehem had broken. Naomi had relatives still living in that city, and so once again, out of the quality of practical wisdom, she resolved to return there. She suggested to her Moabite daughters-in-law that they follow the same principle, that is, go back to their families and seek what protection could be found there.

It is at this juncture of our story that the heroine of this chapter manifests more of the same courage that had enabled her earlier to break with conventional custom and marry outside her racial lines. Here is where the single most famous quotation in the Book of Ruth occurs: "Entreat me not to leave thee, or to return from following after thee: for whither thou goest, I will go; and where thou lodgest, I will lodge. Thy people shall be my people, and thy God my God. Where thou diest, will I die, and there will I be buried: the Lord do so to me, and more also, if aught but death part thee and me" (Ruth 1:17).

One cannot help but wonder what accounted for Ruth's brave and unusual decision to accompany her mother-in-law back to a foreign country. Was it the deep affection that had developed between these two human beings? In the history of the race, mothers-in-law and daughters-in-law have been classic antagonists. Thus, it would be unusual, to say the least, that folk with this kind of native conflictual heritage could have grown so close. Yet, this could be the reason— soul had become so linked with soul that the idea of separation was intolerable.

Another possibility is that Ruth did not have that strong a family system in Moab to which to return. Lois Henderson, in her fictional novel entitled *Ruth,* imagines that the reason Ruth's father agreed for her to marry a Hebrew in the first place was a lack of any real family affection. Thus, it could have been that going back to Israel with Naomi offered the best human prospect open to the widowed Ruth.

However, I think there is still another possibility, and I construe it from one of the phrases in Ruth's famous declaration: "Thy God [shall be] my God." It is entirely possible that in her interaction with a Hebrew family, Ruth the Moabite had begun to glimpse the genuine difference that existed between the religion of Yahweh and the pagan religion that characterized her own family heritage.

Those of us who have been raised in a Judeo-Christian culture sometimes do not realize how unique this particular system is. When the God Yahweh first appeared to Abraham, that forebear must have been astonished beyond measure at a God who wanted to bless rather than to curse! Up until that moment, the basic assumption had been that divinities were either indifferent to humanity or downright hostile.

The ancient myth of Prometheus gives us a glimpse into the world of this pagan mindset. Prometheus was one of the lesser Greek gods who supposedly looked down from Mount Olympus and had compassion on the plight of suffering mortal beings. They were cold and confused in their darkness, so this one took fire from the altar of heaven and gave it as a gift to warm and illumine humankind. When Zeus, the king of the gods, discovered what Prometheus had done, he was infuriated; to show compassion for human beings was a crime against divinity! So Prometheus was punished by being put on an island in the midst of a river and tortured there perennially.

Such images convey the typical way pagan humanity felt about the attitude of heaven. Therefore, to meet a God who wanted to bless human beings and knew how to do it represents an absolute break with the tradition of paganism. The point here is that as Ruth lived in close contact with followers of Yahweh, as she heard them tell and retell their stories of the past, and as she glimpsed the difference the religion of Yahweh made in every facet of their life, a growing intrigue may have built up in her and become her main reason for accompanying Naomi. This would suggest that Ruth's decision represented a religious journey as well as a physical one, and it corresponds beautifully with the promise made to Abraham that eventually all the families of the human race would be able to bless themselves because of him.

I think it is highly likely that Naomi's religion as well as the affection that existed between these two individuals accounts for Ruth's decision. And while Naomi, who knew from her own experience what it was like to go as a foreigner into another country, tried to discourage Ruth from coming with her, she relented when she saw how steadfast her daughter-in-law was in her resolve. The two women, perhaps attaching themselves to one of the caravans of that day, made the journey back west from Moab to Bethlehem.

When they reached the little village south of Jerusalem, Naomi's kinspeople were amazed to see her. She was very direct about what had happened to her. She even suggested that they call her "Mara," which is a term for weeping, rather than Naomi, because in her own words: "The Almighty has dealt very bitterly with me. I went away full, and the Lord has brought me back empty. . . . the Lord has afflicted me and the Almighty has brought calamity upon me" (1:21).

It is so easy for us humans to give a simplistic explanation for what is in fact a very complex situation. It seems here that Naomi saw God as the only Actor in the drama of history and therefore concluded that the tragedies that had occurred in her life emanated solely from what the Holy One did.

The opposite form of this kind of simplicity would be to view oneself as the sole actor in history and therefore to take all the responsibility or blame for what has occurred.

I learned not too long ago in my human pilgrimage that there is a kind of egotism or "dark grandiosity" behind such excessive feelings of guilt. It is almost as if a person says, "I am solely to blame for all of the bad things that have occurred. . . . I am the center of the universe; . . . all events can be traced back to me."

The truth of the matter is that history is a complex interaction of many forces. Simone Weil once said that "creation was the moment that God ceased to be everything so that we humans could become something." That means functionally that in the beginning the Holy One possessed all power, but through creation chose of his own free will to share that potency with others. To use the image of a card game, God "deals" some of his power to many other players, which means history is now the arena where many centers of freedom and power interact. The Holy One is no longer the only One. He has not absented the stage of history and pulled out of the process, but he really has turned over some of his power to other human control.

Therefore, for Naomi to have blamed God as she did for all the things that had happened in Moab was really inappropriate, just as it would have been inappropriate for her to have taken the whole burden of guilt on herself. The depth of her grief was understandable. But as is so often the case, her explanation of why these tragedies had happened leaves something to be desired.

Let it be said in Naomi's defense, however, that though she had her moments of dark bitterness and seeming despair, the kind of wisdom that we have seen throughout this whole chapter manifested itself once again. The two widows returned to Bethlehem just as the barley crop was being harvested, and Ruth, who was no stranger to hard work or resourceful coping, quickly discovered that it was the custom in that land of Yahweh for widows and dependent people to follow the reapers and to pick up what they could from the fields. This was consistent with the Hebrew belief that the Creator really cared for all that he had created—even widows, orphans, and other dependent persons.

So Ruth the Moabite woman began to work in the fields. And Boaz, a wealthy citizen of Bethlehem and a distant kinsman of Elimelech, noticed her in his field one day and sought to learn more about her. Tradition has it that she was an exceedingly beautiful woman. It is also likely that word of what she had done for Naomi had made the rounds in the little village; perhaps this wealthy landowner was impressed that there was nothing dependent or overly self-pitying about this young widow, that she was willing to go to work to do what she could for herself and her mother-in-law. At any rate, he spoke to her in the field and instructed some of his men to deliberately drop some grain for her. That encounter in the field was the beginning of a very significant process that was to place Ruth finally in the most famous lineage of Israel's history.

There was a custom in that day called "levirate marriage," which was designed to insure that widows would be cared for and that descendants would be born in the family line of deceased persons. In such a tradition the male next-of-kin was obligated to take his dead relative's widow as his wife, and with her, if possible, to have children who would be considered descendants and heirs of the dead man.

When Naomi learned about Boaz's inquiries of Ruth, she once again assumed a courageous, proactive stance and guided Ruth into doing something that was as daring in that day as marrying a foreigner. She had Ruth dress in her best and go to the threshing floor where Boaz had been working. In that culture, as in most, working men ate and drank heavily after their labors. Boaz had obviously had his fill of lots of good things and lay down by the threshing floor to sleep. Naomi instructed Ruth to lie down at his feet and, when he awoke the next morning, to remind him of his obligation as a kinsperson to marry her and assure descendants in her husband's family line. In so doing, she would indicate her willingness to pursue the relationship with Boaz.

Such a move could have backfired terribly, but it did not. Could it be that Another, bigger than all of these human actors, was a part of this drama? I think so. Boaz got Ruth's point immediately and must have found the prospect more than a grim duty. He made all the necessary arrangements and took Ruth to be his wife and Naomi under his family care. From this union came Obed, the grandfather of the fabled King David and the ancestor of our Lord himself.

Wisdom, courage, devotion, affection—all of these qualities stand out for us in the story of our foremother Ruth. She really is worthy of the adjective *wise*, as is her mother-in-law Naomi. As much as any others in our heritage, these two women "knew what time it was" in their lives and proceeded to seize those holy opportunities and do what was most appropriate. We could all profit from "going and doing likewise."

Questions for Thought and Discussion

1. What does the word *wise* mean to you? Identify the qualities embodied in such a word.

2. Enumerate the various acts of courage in the life of our foremother Ruth.

3. Why did Ruth choose to remain with Naomi?

4. What are some ways today that adjectives are used as nouns to limit and dehumanize people?

8

SAMUEL
Crossing Where It's Narrow

YOU MAY RECALL very little about the Old Testament character
Samuel, but if you remember anything at all, it may be in
relation to his mother, Hannah, and the events that preceded
his birth. Hannah has become something of a special heroine
for Mother's Day sermons because she fervently prayed for
a child and then, when he was born, gave him back to the
Lord to be raised at the tabernacle in Shiloh. I do not mean
to be iconoclastic here, but I honestly think that when you
get right down to the particulars of the situation, this woman
has been overpraised.

You see, Hannah was married to a prominent man from
Ramah named Elkanah, and she had not been able to bear
him any children. The problem of infertility was regarded
very differently back then than it is today. Ironically, in light
of what we know now, all blame for childlessness was placed
on the woman, and her very worth as a human being was
measured by "failure" in this area.

Here is another manifestation of one of humanity's oldest
problems—making some form of productiveness the basis
of human worth. I was talking to a group of parents recently
about keeping the relation of "being," "doing," "having"
straight in our minds. When the God's gift of "being" is
seen as primal and foundational, then creative "doing" and
responsible "having" grow naturally from such a base. But
when we turn reality upside down and make "doing" or "having" the basis of "being," we produce anxiety and distortion
of the worst kind. Having to produce *or else* is frightening!

This is where Hannah found herself—a female unable to

"produce" in a culture that valued women only on those terms. In desperation she went to the shrine at Shiloh to seek a religious solution to her problem. Notice carefully the shape of her prayer (Sam. 1:11). In effect, Hannah was proposing a bargain with God. If he would open her womb and enable her to do what a woman in that day had to do in order to be accepted, then she would give the child back to God and allow him to come to Shiloh to live and work in that shrine.

Now such a proposal may have a very holy ring on the surface, but deeper down you find a lot of what C. S. Lewis calls "need love." Hannah was concerned here for Hannah— and for her status in the eyes of her husband and the community. Her goal was not so much that God might have another servant on earth as it was that her womanhood might be vindicated. Instead of going to Shiloh and asking God for strength to make the world a better place—that is, overturning this notion that a certain kind of doing is the basis for being—Hannah went seeking simply a better place for herself in the world as it was. "Help me to be a success as the world defines success" was her plea, not, "Transform my sense of what authentic success really is."

What I am saying is that most of the Mother's Day sermons that glorify Hannah's prayer are at best naïve and superficial. Religion for her was a means to certain culturally defined ends rather than a process of understanding the true ends of life and herself becoming a means to those true ends. This is a very common temptation indeed, and who of us has not done the very same thing over and over again? We establish a goal—or more often we let society establish a goal for us—and our praying consists of bargaining with God to help us accomplish this. Biblical religion at its highest is something quite different—letting God help us establish the ends, and then offering ourselves as the means. None of us has the right to throw stones at Hannah, for we have all done the same thing she did. Nonetheless, I want to point out that this is infantile religion at best. It is where we all begin. Hopefully, it is not where Hannah or any of us end up.

However, the beautiful thing about this story is a note you have heard me strike again and again in this book. God took Hannah's situation—selfishness and all—and once again brought something good out of the less-than-perfect. He met Hannah where she was in her cultural captivity and nonetheless brought forth one of the truly great men in all of the Old Testament.

After all, God never has the luxury of pure motives to work with as far as human beings are concerned. Varying mixtures of good and evil are all he ever has at his disposal; the wonder to me is that God could take an anxious conformist like Hannah and bring the likes of Samuel out of her! Does not this offer a basis of hope for all of us—that God can take just about anything and do just about everything with it?

To Hannah's credit, let it be said she did keep her side of the bargain once Samuel had been born. We are not told how hard or how easy such an act of relinquishment was for her. After all, she had accomplished her goal and shed the shame of barrenness. Now she took Samuel, when he was old enough to wean, to the tabernacle in Shiloh and turned him over to Eli the priest that he might become the servant of the Lord.

It was at Shiloh, taught by Eli and sleeping in the same room with the Ark of the Covenant, that Samuel grew up and received the bulk of his significant training. And it was from Shiloh that he moved to become one of the finest characters in the annals of the Old Testament; less negative is said about Samuel than about any other major figure in this whole document. He became the spiritual leader of his people for over forty years, presiding over their feasts, interceding for them before God, and serving as a judge and arbitrator in practical affairs.

An interesting phrase is used to describe Samuel as a young man. It was said that "the Lord . . . did let none of his words fall to the ground" (1 Sam. 3:19, KJV). This means that what he said was wise and full of insight and able to do what it was supposed to accomplish. This image is symbolic of Samuel's whole life; it had real substance and focus from beginning to end. In his birth the Lord accomplished more than giving Hannah the status she so desperately craved. He began a life that can be a model for us if we have the wisdom to perceive and to learn.

There are two things in particular that I find instructive about the life of Samuel. One is the way he developed religiously. Here is a classic example of evolutionary rather than revolutionary religious experience. From the beginning Samuel, like Samson, was exposed to intense religious conditioning, but in his case it "took" and Samuel responded positively. As Harry Emerson Fosdick once put it, "He crossed the stream at the narrowest place." His life with God was one of continuity and steady growth rather than the upheaval and crisis-after-crisis pattern which tends to get so much attention. This is important to note, for what could be called "the Damascus Road syndrome" is far more colorful and, if we are not careful, can get elevated into the single norm of all religious experience.

The way that Samuel grew into God is a good corrective at this point, for early in his pilgrimage he began encountering the Mystery and saying yes. Thus he did not need the kind of radical about-face that someone like the prodigal son in Jesus' parable had to undergo. This is not to imply that there was anything mechanical or automatic about Samuel's religious life. He *did* have to decide for himself at each juncture. When the still, small voice of God impinged upon his consciousness, it was Samuel and not Eli who had to answer. But his answer was affirmative: "Speak, Lord; for thy servant heareth" (1 Sam. 3:9, KJV). This became the pattern of Samuel's whole life, which is undoubtedly why his efforts counted for so much and none of his words "fell to the ground."

A fine Christian woman came to me years ago after a high-powered evangelist had just been in our community. He had had a dramatic conversion from alcoholism late in life, and this woman was questioning the validity of her own religious experience because nothing like that had happened to her. But she had moved step by step with Christ in conscious commitment, and I could say of her, as Marney once said, "A Jesus had been around somewhere in the shaping of this life."

I suggested to this woman that if she could see what she would be like at that moment had she not developed with Christ across the years, then the difference the evangelist was talking about would be apparent. She, like Samuel, had "crossed the stream at the narrowest place" and had experienced the Lord's transforming power gradually, but nonetheless authentically. The evangelist, on the other hand, had waited until the island of his life had drifted far away from the continent of God. No wonder, then, that his journey back across had been more violent.

I believe we need to recognize the validity of both types of experiences and not establish either one as an exclusive norm. Samuel is a prototype of a host of people who early in their lives were given an invitation to the banquet of God and who had the good wisdom to sit down quickly and start making the most of it.

While part of the Good News is the assertion that it is never *too late* to come back, another part of the Good News is the fact that it is never *too early* to begin to take one's place and start to grow. Let's face it; one of the reasons Samuel's words did not "fall to the ground" lies in the fact that he wasted so little of his life at cross-purposes with reality. He was able to accomplish all that he did because he turned early toward the light and walked increasingly into more and more of it. Samuel's pilgrimage was one of steady continuity. It is never too late to start saying yes to God, but then it is never too early, either!

The other thing that I find instructive about Samuel is the way he handled the process of change at the end of his life. He found himself having to live through one of those "hinge eras" in the life of his nation. The children of Israel had lived for two hundred years in Palestine in a loosely organized fashion, but gradually the Philistines had developed into a monarchy and learned to make weapons of iron. Thus they threatened to put the Hebrews right back into the slave situation from which they had fled out of Egypt.

The loose political structure of Israel was no match for this new challenge, any more than the scattered Indian tribes in this country were a match for organized Westerners, and so the possibility of Israel moving into a monarchial form of government was raised. At first Samuel was offended by such an idea. It amounted to a rejection of his own leadership and a departure from that direct dependence on God that had been so central to Israel's life. Samuel's initial reaction was a negative, conservative one, but here is what I admire about him: *He did not stop there.*

Samuel recognized that something genuinely new had

emerged, and try as he would to look back, he realized that the simpler structures of old were not adequate for the challenge of the new. So, through genuine struggle, Samuel is depicted as doing an awesome thing—*he changed his mind.* Reluctantly he let go the beloved old ways and voluntarily embraced the new.

We all witnessed this sort of thing happening in the South in the last thirty years, as a certain way of doing life between blacks and whites has had to give way to another. There are always extremists on both sides of such a process—those who refuse to budge an inch and those who have so little sense of any value to conserve that they would "throw out the baby with the bathwater." What I like most about Samuel is that he was not an extremist in either direction. He loved the old ways, as well he should have, but he also saw where history was moving and what had to be done lest everything be lost.

A minister friend of mine once lived through the experience of a tornado's striking his town, and he learned a lesson from it that was telling indeed. The only things that managed to survive, he noted, had two qualities: foundations and flexibility. If there was no secure grounding or connection with the earth, the structure blew away. By the same token, if there was no give—that is, if something were utterly rigid— the structure was demolished. He went on to say that the same qualities are essential for both the people and the institutions who are called on to live amid the high winds of change. And this is exactly what I see Samuel doing so well; he had firm rootage in the past, but he was flexible as well.

If you and I are going to survive in the kind of world in which we live, neither absolute conservatism nor total iconoclasm is likely to work. Roots and flexibility—these are the crucial qualities, and the way Samuel handled the last challenge of his life is in its own way as impressive as the way he began.

Questions for Thought and Discussion

1. How do you feel about Hannah's plight and the measures she took to cope with it?

2. Which type of religious development best describes your pilgrimage—evolutionary or revolutionary?

3. Name an instance in your own life when a good deed done for selfish motives has nevertheless had positive results. Have there been other instances where less-than-pure motives seemed to "spoil" the good deed? How would such instances affect your view about God being able to bring "something good out of something less than perfect"?

4. Can you name certain people you know whose words "do not fall to the ground" because of the lives behind them? Who are they?

5. Amid the high winds of culture change, where do you most need to grow—in foundations or in flexibility?

9

SAUL
Learning to Take Our Place

OF ALL THE HUMAN ACTIONS that upset us and disturb us, a suicide is one of the most extreme. Whenever this tragedy happens within our family circle or to someone we know, it sets off a flood of questions and somber soul searching. We cannot help but ask why such a thing occurred . . . or what went wrong . . . who failed somehow? We may try to evade such questions by attributing the suicide to insanity or madness, but this will usually not satisfy us for long. Something deep within us wants an explanation for this most ultimate rejection of life.

Unhappily, this is the kind of inquiry that stands before us now, for the ancestor who is the subject of this chapter was a suicide—he took his own life by deliberately falling on his sword in the heat of a losing battle. I am referring, of course, to Saul, the first king of Israel, and the tragedy of the way he ended his life is heightened by the brilliance of his beginning. At the outset of his career, Saul, the son of Kish, seemed to possess all of the ingredients necessary for a successful life. He was an impressive man physically—handsome, and literally head and shoulders taller than the average Hebrew. He was also deeply religious, humble, courageous in battle, and had that charismatic flair that enabled him to inspire other people to action. And he was able to achieve a great deal during the years of his reign. At a time when the children of Israel were sinking back into slavery and were at their lowest ebb since entering Palestine, he fired their spirits again and rolled back their enemies from the central highlands of the Promised Land.

All in all, Saul had a great deal going for him, both in terms of natural gifts and achievement. Why, then, did he wind up a suicide, an utterly defeated and embittered man? It is an inquiry we would do well to pursue, for he was one of our forebears, and examples do not have to be positive for us to learn something constructive from them. Thus, let us try to penetrate the tragic shadows that surround Saul's life and to untangle for our own enlightenment the events that led up to this failure.

Let me identify at least three things that perhaps contributed to his undoing. First of all, the despair that settled over Saul at the end of his life may have resulted partly from some unrealistic expectations he had for the office of kingship in Israel. You may remember from the previous chapter what a radical thing it was for the Hebrews to establish a monarchy. They had never had much internal organization. Their life in the Promised Land still bore the marks of the fierce independence that characterized their life in the desert, and there was much in their tradition to militate against a human king with ongoing authority. Yahweh had been their only King, and their leaders had been those heroes he would raise up periodically in the midst of crisis.

Yet we also saw in the previous chapter that the Philistines now posed a brand-new threat to Israel. Here was an organized military state with a standing army bent on expansionistic aggression. The old institutions of a tribal league and a volunteer militia were no match for such a threat, and this realization, more than anything else, is what led Samuel and the rest of the nation reluctantly to establish a monarchy around young Saul.

It is clear from the several accounts that exist side-by-side in 1 Samuel that Saul did not seek the job of king, but that when it came to him he saw the need and set out to do something about it. But perhaps in doing so he dreamed too idealistically, failing to reckon with the slow pace and great agony that always characterize significant social change. Genuine alterations in the fabric of society rarely happen swiftly in our world, and perhaps Saul was naïve at this point. All through his reign he experienced opposition and conflict to the idea of kingship, even from Samuel and some of the very ones who had supported it at first. It could be that Saul was unprepared for such a slow process and fell victim to his own unrealistic and disappointed idealism.

Experiences like this can breed despair—when one does not reckon with the distance between "one's reach and one's grasp," to use Robert Browning's term. St. Paul once acknowledged that we humans "know in part and prophesy in part," that our seeing is as "through a glass, darkly" (1 Cor. 13:9, 12, kjv). We need to realize that such partialness is not confined to the realm of knowledge alone; it also pertains to our achieving as well. It might just as well have been written that "we achieve in part," that is, what we actually accomplish is usually only a fraction of what we would like to have done. In reality the institution of kingship did not get fully established in Israel for almost fifty years after Saul's reign. It was not until Solomon that the structure of centralized authority really came into its own. Saul's reign was only the first step in a long and involved process that took decades to complete, and part of Saul's problem may have been that he failed to realize this fact and judged his achievements by far too high a standard.

Disillusionment is almost always the child of illusion. Start with a wrong assumption and you are sure to end up with a mistaken conclusion. I believe this was one of Saul's problems. He did not realize the partialness of all human accomplishments. Who of us ever fulfills our fondest dreams totally or completely? We each need to realize that at best we are a tiny part of a great process that flows both before us and on after us. We have a part to play, but not a total part, and wise is the one who senses this and comes to terms with it. Apparently, Saul never did this, which may be why he seemed more of a failure to himself than he really was.

A second contributing factor to Saul's tragic end may have been the kind of support Saul received after becoming king—particularly the imbalance between criticism and counsel. Once again, we need to remember that Saul came along at a particularly difficult moment in the transition of Israel. The oppression of the Philistines made the office of kingship a necessity, yet no one had any experience in this area or knew what to do. The old judge Samuel came nearer than anyone to being an expert in national leadership, but he was at best half-hearted about the shift to monarchy. Once Saul had been anointed king, Samuel did not really help him find his way on this new frontier of leadership. In fact, what we see here is what so often happens in life. A person is given a difficult job by a group and, instead of struggling with him, the group sits back and lets him struggle alone, until at last he hangs himself. At that point they move in and reject him—when it is too late to salvage anything.

You will remember that I lauded Samuel for his ability to change with the times and accept a monarchy, but I cannot laud him for the way he carried through on that decision. He really did not give Saul the kind of help he needed for this most difficult task. What Samuel did give was criticism and negative judgment and rejection after the fact.

It is little wonder that Saul felt undermined and betrayed by the very one who had put him into office. After all, if the only form of interest people take in us is criticism, their interest can be devastating. If you see me struggling with a problem and truly want to help me with it, then your negative insights into what I am doing may well be constructive. If I feel that you are somehow in the problem with me, your opinions—even critical ones—can be helpful. If, on the other hand, I never hear from you until it is too late, and you come in with nothing but condemnation and rejection, you simply add to my problem and make an already difficult situation worse.

We will see in the next chapter that Saul's successor to the throne, King David, had a forthright critic in the prophet Nathan, but he worked *with* David in the midst of his problem and in the name of redemption, rather than waiting until the die was cast and then pronouncing doom. If Samuel had given the kind of sympathetic counsel to Saul that later Nathan gave to David, who knows? Saul's career might have been different.

Saul was teachable as a young man. The record of his life gives every evidence that he was open to direction as he struggled with decisions. He was also capable of repentance and willing to admit when he was wrong. Perhaps Samuel's own bias against a monarchy got in the way here and made him a little hopeful that Saul would fail. At any rate, all the inexperienced king got from his supporters was criticism and rejection. If only there had been counsel and advice in the midst of the process, things might have been different.

This is something all parents and administrators and supervisors of any sort would do well to note. If we really want those under our care to succeed, we must relate to them with something other than criticism, and we must deal with them during the process, not after it is all over. William Penn once said, "He has a right to censure who has a heart to help," and this is so true. If our criticisms are to be of any benefit, they must come at a different time and spring from different motives than did the advice Saul received. When all is said and done, the tragedy that came to Saul was partly due to the kind of support he received from others; it came too late and was all criticism and no counsel.

And yet, I doubt if this failure would have had such an impact on Saul if it had not been for a third factor, which was Saul's inadequate view of himself and of his place in the economy of God's purpose. For some reason, Saul was never able fully to accept who he was and what he was supposed to do under God. He never found the security to say, "By the grace of God, I am *what* I am and I am *where* I am." He never seemed to see himself as a gifted person, an instrument of God created by the Lord for a specific task. Therefore, he was never able to take his place in the world—that place "prepared for him before the foundations of the earth." And I believe this inability, this identity problem, lies at the root of Saul's ultimate undoing. Samuel Miller once said quite perceptively that "our peace is in our place," and Saul was never able to come to a positive sense of that reality.

The first hint of this inability to be himself appears in what looks like modesty and a genuine sense of humility. When approached by Samuel to be anointed king, Saul was surprised and disclaimed any fitness for this kind of role. This sort of response would be appropriate if this were another human being trying to force on another a false identity. But remember, this was actually the call of God, the challenge of him who had fashioned Saul for this task. And what appeared at first as acceptable modesty finally emerged as Saul's major flaw—he would never be himself or take the place for which he was intended.

This problem showed itself in two extreme forms during

Saul's lifetime. On the one hand, it caused him to under-reach, to be too hesitant and too dependent on others. Instead of being sure of his own giftedness and asserting this with clarity, Saul allowed himself to be overinfluenced by others and thrown off the path of obedience.

For example, after Saul had assumed the kingship and won a preliminary battle with the Philistines, the enemy gathered their forces at Michmash. The stage was set for a big confrontation. Saul had rallied his army and was waiting for Samuel to come and offer a sacrifice to consecrate the effort. However, Samuel did not show up as he had promised, and tension began to mount, with the enemy poised across the valley and Israelites beginning to defect.

In light of such a situation, Saul made a sound decision. Rather than wait any longer and lose his army or go into battle unconsecrated, he ordered the lamb brought to him as God's leader and offered the sacrifice himself. As he was finishing the ceremony, Samuel arrived and became incensed that Saul had gone ahead. It was obvious that Samuel was defensive about his own priestly duties and did not want the new king encroaching on them. Instead of standing his ground, however, and reminding Samuel that he was the one who had defaulted, Saul wilted and pulled back in, showing that tragic lack of clarity as to who he was and what he ought to do that was always to hamper him. Again and again Saul let other people deflect him from "doing his thing" under God, and this hesitant insecurity contributed to his downfall.

Ironically, this same security problem that sometimes caused Saul to underreach also caused him to *overreach* on other occasions, to defend what did not need to be defended. If our place is created for us by God, we do not have to fight to keep it, any more than we have to fight to create it; it is ours for the assuming. But Saul did not grasp this, and so toward the end of his life he fell into a jealousy of David that ultimately destroyed him.

If one is secure in his or her place, then one can let others be what they are and look on them as allies and helpers, which is exactly what David was to Saul. A skillful musician, a great warrior, an utterly loyal subject—he should have been numbered among Saul's greatest blessings. But to one who was not sure of himself, David became just the opposite—a threat and an enemy. The same reason that kept Saul from taking his place in the world made him fearful that someone else would, and so he became absolutely paranoid, turning from his real enemies—the Philistines—to one that was not an enemy at all—his colleague, David.

This dividing of the house against itself severely weakened Israel at a time she needed to be strong and led Saul to embark finally on the ill-conceived battle that ended in his hopeless defeat and suicide. There toward the end, Saul seems to have become actually insane; at the time of his death he was literally "beside himself." And this phrase, better than any other, sums up Saul's basic problem. He somehow had never been willing to be himself; instead, he was always "beside himself"—outside the place which had been provided for him from the foundations of the earth. And this, more than anything else, I believe, accounts for his tragic failure.

It is important that we look long at this phenomenon, for the point of Saul's undoing is a point at which all of us are vulnerable. Back of much of the hesitant conformity and insecure jealousy of our day stands this same yawning chasm— our unwillingness to be ourselves and to occupy "the place that is our peace." Self-doubt, which grows into self-despising, is the root problem behind so many of our present-day disorders, and nothing short of hearing Genesis 1 as the account of our own creation can answer such a need.

Listen! You are here because God wants you to be here. Before the foundation of the earth, it was decided that you would be you and occupy your particular place in the great drama creation. You did not earn this place, nor can anyone take it away from you. "Your peace is in your place"—God's gift to you and you alone.

If Saul could have seen himself in this light, what a difference it would have made. With that, he could have handled his own achievements more gracefully and allowed the criticism and lack of support he received to be what it was— his critics' problem and no reflection on his worth. But he did not love himself aright; he never affirmed in the depth of his soul that most basic truth of all: "By the grace of

God, I am *what* I am, and am *where* I am." That is the place where our peace is. To be "beside" that is to miss it. To be there—gratefully and realistically—is to have found life's most basic secret.

Questions for Thought and Discussion

1. What feelings in you does an event of suicide evoke?

2. Which has been a greater problem for you—what you expect of yourself or what others expect of you?

3. When, if ever, is criticism genuinely constructive?

4. Think of an instance from your own experience in which jealousy threatened or destroyed a relationship. Do you feel that insecurity or lack of self-acceptance played an important part in this situation?

5. What forces within you work against an act of genuine self-acceptance?

10

DAVID
Getting Ourselves Off Our Hands

THERE IS AN OLD ADAGE in nautical circles to the effect that "no sailor ever distinguished himself on a smooth sea." What we call human greatness is never achieved apart from difficulty and conflict. The book of Hebrews says that Jesus was made perfect by the things he suffered (2:11), and there seems to be no other way in this kind of world. Pressure and adversity have a way of bringing to the surface the best that is in a person, and this is certainly true of the ancestor to which we now turn—our forebear David.

I once did an extensive study of David in a little book, now out of print, called *Stages: The Art of Living the Expected.* However, I feel the lessons that are "fleshed out" in this one's life are so important that I decided to risk repeating myself slightly and include some of them here also. Therefore, let us turn to one of the genuine heroes of the Old Testament.

Alongside Abraham and Moses, David is probably the best known of all our spiritual ancestors, a man who became literally "a legend in his own time." Here was one who took over after Saul's disastrous attempt to be Israel's first king and, in less than forty years, not only united Israel as a nation but made her the dominant force from the Nile to the Euphrates—clearly the most powerful nation in the Near East. This was an incredible accomplishment, and yet at the same time David was perennially besieged by problems and difficulties. The sea on which David had to sail was anything but smooth; he lived in conflict practically all the waking hours of his life. For me, at least, this makes what he accomplished that much more impressive.

You are probably aware that David began his career on a brilliant note. One day he was an unheralded keeper of sheep, and the next day he was catapulted to fame by killing the giant Goliath. He was a skilled musician and poet as well as a courageous warrior, and very soon he was taken into the royal family as the apple of the king's eye, successively becoming Saul's armor-bearer, then his son-in-law, and finally the commander-in-chief of all Saul's troops.

However, given the insecurity of the king's makeup, nothing failed like success, and David fell into disfavor as quickly as he had risen to prominence. He soon became the object of the king's paranoidal rage. Saul could not bear to hear people sing, "Saul hath slain his thousands, but David his ten thousands," and despite repeated efforts on David's part to assure Saul of his loyalty, he finally had to flee from Saul and began to live the life of a hunted fugitive. Things got so bad that David eventually had to seek sanctuary with the age-old enemies of Israel, the Philistines, and life for him became one precarious escape after another.

This was a drastic switch from the role of court favorite and national hero, and because it was so utterly undeserved in terms of what David had done, lesser persons than he might have collapsed right then and there in bitterness and despair or fear. But it is right at this point that the qualities of true greatness began to show through in David. He did not collapse or say, as Saul would eventually say, "Poor me! Ain't it awful! Stop the world; I want to get off." No, with a quality I call "the courage to cope," David proceeded to make wise and ingenious use of the hand life was dealing him.

He established himself in a desert hideout called Ziklag and began to lash to himself an assortment of folk who for one reason or another were at odds with society. Years later, when Saul fell on his own sword in a tragically ill-conceived battle, the men of Judah, David's home territory, asked him to become their king. Seven years later the northern tribes that Saul had ruled did the same thing. And David proceeded from that point to conquer fully for the first time the land promised to Abraham, then to extend the boundaries of that kingdom to the north and east and south.

This was a real achievement, any way you want to look

at it, yet things did not go smoothly for David, even after he had "made it." He had to fight successive battles with the Philistines, the Ammonites, the Moabites, the Edomites, and the Syrians. And then there was the trauma of his involvement with Bathsheba and the sins of his children that continued to plague him throughout his whole life. At no time was this highly successful man ever free of pressure or difficulty; there were no "smooth seas" in his lifetime.

David became the person he was against tremendous odds and in the face of seemingly insurmountable problems, and understanding how he was able to do all this is the purpose of this chapter. This thing called "the courage to cope" is a much-needed reality. What can we learn from the experience of David that might help bring this kind of courage into the circle of our lives as well?

If I had to sum up David's secret in one sentence, I would put it this way: *he had succeeded in getting himself off his hands.* That most basic of all human problems—the ego problem—seems to have been resolved creatively by him. David was able to view himself as a means, not an end, in life—as instrumental rather than ultimate, as belonging to and serving a purpose larger than his own existence. And this was a key reason he was able to accomplish what he did.

The personnel manager of a national corporation once shared with me some insights which have been pivotal in my personal journey. This man drew a distinction between two basic kinds of persons: those who want most "to be something" and those whose primary desire is "to do something." He said he always made it his number-one goal to quickly find out which kind of person each new executive trainee was, for he had found that this had a direct effect on job performance.

In this man's view, those persons who were intent on "being something" were those who did not have their ego-needs met healthily. Thus, they tended to use the job to enhance themselves. They asked in every situation, "How can I turn this event to my advantage and make it a stepping stone in my career?" "Obviously," the personnel manager said, "these kinds of persons can never risk anything or make a hard decision. Their vision is severely limited by self-concern."

On the other hand, those people who were intent on "do-

ing something" did have their ego-needs met healthily. They
were the ones who were able to ask at a given moment,
"What needs to be done here, irrespective of the impact
on me?" This frame of reference is different from that of
the one who has to "be something" in that something larger
than self is seen as the end, and that self is seen as the means
to that end. "People who think this way," the personnel manager concluded, "are infinitely more valuable and productive
to the company than those who are concerned primarily with
themselves."

I find this distinction at the heart of what made David
what he was. More than any other person in Scripture save
Jesus himself, David was preeminently the kind of person
who wanted "to do something," rather than "be something."
He saw himself as belonging to and being the instrument
of Something larger than himself. This was the source of
his "courage to cope," his magnanimity to Saul, his ability
to make decision after decision in his reign that worked to
the good of the larger reality rather than simply to his own
private good.

Take, for example, his decision to make Jerusalem the capital city of Israel. David had been king of the tribes in the
south for seven years before the tribes in Saul's old territory
asked him to rule them as well. That was a tremendous step
for old antagonists to take, and a person who needed to
"be something" would have grasped the occasion to drama-
tize his victory by making his capital of Hebron the seat of
the government and advertising to all the world that the
northern tribes had come to him.

But David did not have those dominant needs. Remember,
he saw himself as belonging to and being the instrument
of Something larger than himself, so he did an absolutely
ingenious thing. He captured the city of Jerusalem, an old
Jebusite stronghold that none of the tribes of Israel had ever
been able to conquer, and he made that neutral site the center
for uniting the nation. This way, no part of Israel was humiliated, and all were given a sense of a new beginning. This
is how folk who primarily want "to do something" tend to
work—efficiently in terms of the common good.

This leads to the question: "How did David get himself
off his hands, or find a way to meet his ego-needs so healthily

that he did not have to resort to using each situation to enhance himself?" Those of you who know me may well anticipate my answer here, for if there is one note I have struck more often than any other, it is this one: *David's ego-needs were loved off his hands, not despised away or worked off by any strenuous effort of his own.* It has taken me so long to begin to understand this process. I used to look down on ego-needs and feel there was something wrong with thinking of self at all. For a long time my goal was to be totally oblivious to self. But I have begun to learn how humanly impossible this is—not to mention being contrary to the Christian gospel as well.

I have come to see that our egos are like our physical bodies—they have to be fed in some way. If I decided that hunger was a sin and that the way to handle hunger was to ignore it or shame myself for feeling hungry, you know what would happen: the desire for food would come to dominate my whole consciousness. "Men do live by bread alone when they are starving," says Abraham Maslow. When a need is not acknowledged and cared for properly, it grows into an obsession. And this is what happens to ego-needs when they are ignored or neglected. The issue is not whether "ego hunger" is right or wrong, but whether the sort of "food" we are giving it has the power to satisfy this hunger healthily and help us grow.

My contention is that early in his life David found the diet that made for ego-health, and it was summed up in these words, "It is he that hath made us, and not we ourselves" (Ps. 100:3). David recognized the most basic fact about himself—that he was a creature birthed and held in existence by the action of Another, not something that had created or could create himself. And this is why he did not have to spend his life trying "to be something." By the grace of God, he already was something; he belonged to and was the instrument of Somebody larger than himself. Thus he was free to be a means to that One's ends, "to do something" in that One's service because the "being" issue was already resolved.

David's life was clearly in the One who had made him, not in what he had to make of himself. You can see that in the way he danced himself into a frenzy when the symbol of God's presence—the Ark of the Covenant—was brought back to Jerusalem, or in those majestic words of his in Psalm 103: "Bless the Lord, O my soul: and all that is within me, bless his holy name." I am convinced this was the source of David's "courage to cope"—how he got himself off his hands, how he was able to strive to "do something" instead of "be something" and thereby to accomplish so much.

And David's secret is an open one—available to you and to me and to everyone. We will never ignore—or despise or even work—ourselves off our hands. There is only one way that self can ever be healthily denied or taken away, and that is by letting God *love* it off our hands.

I repeat: David's secret is an open secret. What was true of him is true of you and me as well: "It is he who hath made us, and not we ourselves." We too are "his people, and the sheep of his pasture" (Ps. 100:3). We do not have to earn our worth or justify our existence by our efforts. That issue is already settled by virtue of who made us. The only question for each of us is: "Will I accept this, and glory in it, and go forth to do something because I already am something in God's sight?"

Questions for Thought and Discussion

1. Where did David begin his life journey, and what different things did he do along the way to becoming a famous king?

2. What do you think was the secret of David's singular greatness?

3. How do any of us go about "getting ourselves off our hands"?

4. What have you discovered about the relation of adversity to achievement?

11

SOLOMON
Lesson for the Second Half of Life

WITH THE COMING OF SOLOMON to rule as the third king of Israel, a distinctive era in the history of the people of God came to an end. In an economic and political sense, the reign of Solomon marked the fulfillment of the promise to Abraham. All Palestine now was under the control of the Hebrews, and they were unquestionably the grandest and the most influential power of that day.

In another sense, however, the rule of Solomon marked the end of the heroic period of Israel's life. Her national pilgrimage had been something like a Horatio Alger saga. She had come up from the oppression of slavery in Egypt, had moved through the relatively simple days of living in the wilderness, and had gradually infiltrated the Promised Land. Her life back then was very primitive. The only leaders were the heroes God would raise up in emergencies, and her only government was loyalty to the covenant with Yahweh made in Sinai.

All that was swept away, however, by the time Solomon had finished his reign. He had not come to power as a charismatic leader, but rather as part of a dynastic process in which the king designated his successor. A temple had been erected in Jerusalem in place of the moving tent by which the God of Exodus had led his people. The territories of the twelve tribes were now divided into administrative districts for the purpose of taxation and conscription and defense. In short, the kingship of Solomon marked a real junction in the life of the people of Israel.

Throughout this volume, I have emphasized what the Bible

makes no attempt to hide: that all our forebears were mixed creatures, paradoxical blends of weaknesses and strengths. And King Solomon, for all his fabled glory, is no exception. There is much in this man's life to be admired and emulated, and yet there is also a terrifying dimension to be noted and avoided if at all possible.

On the positive side of Solomon's life, there are two outstanding characteristics to be underlined. The first of these is the beautiful way that Solomon began his reign. Remember, Solomon had ascended the throne differently than all the other leaders of Israel had. He was no warrior-hero like Gideon or Samson or Saul. Rather, he was the son whom David single-handedly designated to follow him to the throne. The elders of Israel and Judah had not been present when this was done, nor had they participated in this decision. A power struggle had gone on inside the palace, and it had been the dying king who "put the finger" on Solomon and thus made him king.

The whole circumstances surrounding Solomon's coming to power were thus problematic, and of all the steps that the young king could have taken in such a situation, Solomon chose the very best. In a well-known incident, God appeared to him in a dream and asked what he wanted more than anything else.

This age-old test was really a device of discovering a person's true nature. If all possibilities are open to a person, what he or she decides is an accurate reflection of what that one is like on the inside, what his or her true values are. And in response to such a test, Solomon came through with flying colors, for he knew himself and his situation well enough to realize what he needed most. In the moment when he could have had anything in the world, he asked for the wisdom to rule the people aright, that is, to do the job that destiny had laid upon him.

When you stop and think about it, is not wisdom the most crucial of all the things a human being needs? To know how to be one's true self and to do those things that the circumstances of life lay upon one is the finest gift of all, and Solomon is to be commended for recognizing this fact so early in his personal pilgrimage. Most of us only come to this realization far into our adulthood. Fame, money, power, physical satisfaction—these are the goals to which we tend to aspire in the early stages of our life, and it is only after we have experienced how little satisfaction these things really bring that we begin to desire wisdom above all else.

Solomon was genuinely precocious in recognizing so early his need for understanding and discernment, and the Scriptures indicate that God was utterly pleased with his choice. Wisdom is something God wants to give us in abundance; we do not have to cajole or beat it out of him. But consistent with his noncoercive nature, he will not force wisdom on us against our will. If we want anything more than his good will for us, God generally allows us to have it, only to experience in ourselves how much less this is than what he wants for us. Like the Israelites, who "tempted God in the wilderness" until he gave them what they thought they wanted, we find that the natural outcome of getting our desires is "leanness [in our] souls" (Ps. 106:15–16, KJV).

Solomon did not make this mistake, however, and what a lesson there is to be learned here, if we would only heed it! Wisdom—the ability to discern correctly what to do and how to do it—this is the virtue above all virtues, and Solomon went straight for it at the beginning of his life. All his subsequent achievements root in this one seminal choice—let all who have eyes and ears of the heart take note!

The other thing I find admirable about Solomon is the attitude he assumed toward the past and his connection with it. He knew that he owed his opportunity to be king solely to the efforts of his father. Had it not been for David's military exploits or his decision to designate Solomon as his successor, this one would not have been where he was. Thus, in grateful recognition of this fact, Solomon set about to extend and develop more fully the dreams that were dominant in his heritage. He was aware that the great desire of his father's heart had been to build a temple for his God. It had bothered David that he lived in a palace of great splendor while the Ark of the Covenant remained in a tent. In deference to David, and as a symbol of recognition for his connectedness with the past, Solomon made building a temple the first item on his agenda. He spent seven years bringing this dream of his father's to reality.

I like this sense of kinship between one generation and

another, for I think it is true to the nature of this existence of ours. No individual is an island unto himself or herself. We do not begin out of nothing, but enter a stream of connectedness that flows from a distant past. To live for a single moment is to be in constant interaction between the dead and the living and the yet unborn. Edmund Burke used to say that we are "part of an ongoingness"; I believe we need to recognize this fact and act accordingly.

I have chosen to emphasize this sense of connectedness with other generations because I think we need its corrective power just now. Alienation rather than continuity tends to characterize the way today's younger people feel toward older folk. While there may be some legitimate reasons for this attitude, it represents a sickness when allowed to go too far. Rare, indeed, today are a young people who, like Solomon, look with gratitude toward their past and make it a life goal to develop more fully the dreams of their fathers and mothers. Instead, the tendency today is either to curse one's parents or to simply ignore the heritage of the past as if it were of no value at all.

Such "momentariness" is not only the grossest kind of ingratitude; it is also pathetically arrogant and unrealistic. Like it or not, the present does rest on the past, and the attitude we should assume toward this is one of neither total rejection nor total acceptance. Solomon accepted with thankfulness his inheritance of the past and then did his part in developing it more fully. He took his father's unfulfilled dreams and used his life to move them toward completion. In my judgment, this is how we ought to use our "threescore and ten." There should be not only gratitude for what we receive from the past but also responsibility for what we pass on to the future. Solomon, as a good steward of the dynamics of history, has much to teach us here.

I repeat, then: there is much to admire in this man called Solomon. Yet honesty will not permit me to stop here. There was in this one's life a terrifying dimension as well, and I would be amiss if I did not point it out to you as clearly as I underlined his strengths.

To put the whole situation in a nutshell, Solomon ended his life very differently than he began it. I have already noted that the favor of God surrounded those beginning days when

Solomon asked for wisdom and set about to extend the thrust
of the heritage that lay behind him. But then something happened. The eleventh chapter of 1 Kings puts it this way:
"When Solomon was old his wives turned away his heart
after other gods" (v. 4).

This is a haunting statement in two regards. First, look
at *when* it happened. There is a prevalent but very naïve
notion that all crucial decisions in life are made "in the morning" of our lives—that time when we separate from our families of origin, choose a vocation, pick a mate, and so forth.
But this is not the whole truth. All four quarters of the game
of life are significant, and the need to keep on growing is
constant. Carlyle Marney used to say that *continuing* education
is the only kind of education there is, and I would say that
about the whole business of human growth.

To think that one has "arrived" and does not need to
keep on "asking" and "seeking" and "knocking" is tragic
indeed, yet this seems to be what Solomon did. In his old
age he stopped doing life with the intensity and care that
he had brought to his earlier stages. He let down his guard
and began to drift, and what happened? When he was old,
he allowed his heart to be turned away to follow other gods.

I am appalled, then, at *when* this happened, and I take it
as a real warning to someone like me who is just leaving
"the dangerous forties" and entering "the fateful fifties."
What occurred is also significant. What was behind this image
of "following after other gods"? The evidence points in several directions here. For example, affluence, luxuries, and
an absorption with material things seem to have played a
major role in Solomon's spiritual defection.

Perhaps it all began quite innocently as Solomon set about
the task of building the temple unto the Lord. He got very
involved with precious materials during that process, and it
may be that during this time material things gradually ceased
to be the means by which he lived and became the ends
for which he lived. A clue that such a thing was happening
lies in the fact that, after taking only seven years to build
the temple, Solomon spent thirteen years building his own
palace!

From that point on, Solomon's materialism began to escalate. He became obsessed with building and acquiring and

possessing and enlarging. To show you how extensive this obsession became, Solomon wound up enslaving 153,000 people—many of them native-born Israelites—to furnish the labor supply for his extensive building projects. It was an awesome return to the very kind of situation from which Israel had been freed by Yahweh some four hundred years before. And it all happened because, when he was old, Solomon experienced a profound apostasy that involved turning his back on Yahweh and embracing the vision of many gods that touched him through the influence of his non-Hebrew wives.

Such apostasy is no incidental matter when it comes to the dynamics of behavior. Never forget: we humans will always reflect the image of the god we worship. There is tremendous creative power in ultimate devotion. We tend to take on the qualities of that which is most important to us. Thus, when Solomon was young and utterly open to Yahweh and to other people, he was a sensitive and insightful responder to human need—as his handling of the famous case between the two harlots reveals. But when a love of material things began to escalate, and many concerns divided his heart, the kind of hardness and insensitivity that is a characteristic of the inorganic began to characterize Solomon's behavior. He could enslave a vast segment of his own people—why? Because he had become a thing himself, and was willing to use people to enhance the material side of life rather than using things to enhance the human side. The acid test in this area is always the single question: What will you sacrifice—things for the enhancement of persons, or persons for the enhancement of things?

Solomon did a one-hundred-eighty-degree shift here from the God who values persons over things to the god who valued things over persons. And is there any one of us, in this most affluent society the world has ever known, who can be complacent before such an image? I, for one, cannot, and it is to this side of the Solomon story that I would point as we end this chapter. How well he began the race, how wisely he played quarters one and two of the game of life. "But when he was old," says the Book, something happened; he allowed his heart to be turned after other gods.

I do not want this to happen to me, to you, to any of us.

And it does not have to happen—unless we stop growing, stop asking and seeking and knocking, stop analyzing "the affection of our hearts" to see who or what is really god.

Someday, with the gods we have made, we will come face to face with the God who has made us. And only in that moment will the question "Who is your God?" be finally settled. Pray with me that, unlike Solomon, we will find that our god and the real God will be the same.

Questions for Thought and Discussion

1. If you were offered your "heart's desire" in the form of three wishes, what would they be? Would your answer have been different at another stage of your life?

2. What values did your family most cherish? How do you relate to those values now?

3. What is the relative significance of "the afternoon of life" when compared to "the morning" and "the evening"? At which stage do you think you are?

4. Identify the various ways that apostasy or turning after other gods is happening in our time and culture.

1 Kings 17:1–2 Kings 2:14

12

ELIJAH

Good News for Our Down Times

In the long memory of the people of God, few individuals have made as dramatic an impact as the prophet Elijah. This is indicated by the fact that so many accounts of miraculous deeds cluster about him. Almost nothing that he did was ordinary or predictable; he possessed that special charisma that made for daring and exciting action. To this day, it is Elijah whom the Jewish people expect to return and announce the coming of the Messiah. At their Passover celebration the door is still left open for him, and a place is always set for him at the table. In terms of sheer drama, we have no more colorful kinsperson in all our background than this particular individual.

What, then, was Elijah like? For one thing, he was a man of extraordinary courage. Again and again, as he walks the pages of the Old Testament, he is depicted as having that rare ability to thrust himself into threatening situations and to endure tensions that would have immobilized lesser persons. The first glimpse that we get of him in the Scripture is of a rugged man living in a most dangerous way—out alone in the wilds of nature (1 Kings 17:1–7). When we stop to realize that at the time, because of wild animals, bandits, and other enemies, people only moved about in clan groupings, we get some inkling of the courage it took to survive in that lonely setting. Like his ancestor Abraham, Elijah was one of history's first true individualists, a man who dared to set out on his own.

Elijah had another kind of courage as well—the courage to go against prevailing customs and norms. This is illustrated in the well-known incident that occurred while Elijah was boarding with a widow in Phoenicia (1 Kings 17:8–24). One day the widow's son became ill and stopped breathing. Elijah took the boy up on the roof and not only prayed for him, but proceeded to engage in some sort of mouth-to-mouth resuscitation—a practice unheard of in an era when everyone was frightened of corpses and refused even to touch a dead body.

You see, Elijah was bold where other persons were cowardly—and not only with wild animals and corpses, but also with kings and pagan prophets. He happened to have lived during the reign of one of the most powerful rulers of the northern kingdom of Israel—a king named Ahab. And Elijah made no attempt to hide his disagreements with the policies of the throne. When the two of them happened to meet face to face one day on a road, Ahab recognized Elijah and addressed him as the "troubler of Israel"—that is, one who was "rocking the boat" and daring to oppose the king. However, instead of being intimidated by the king's attitude, Elijah answered right back, "You are wrong, Ahab, it is *you* who are troubling Israel with your apostasy" (1 Kings 18:17–18, paraphased).

Out of that meeting came the challenge for the most famous event of Elijah's life, his contest on Mount Carmel with the prophets of Baal. It was what you might call "a theological showdown or shoot-out" to determine which was the real God after all—Yahweh or Baal. All of Israel was summoned to the mountain. On one side were four hundred fifty prophets representing Baal, and on the other side stood one lonely figure—the man Elijah. However, Elijah not only stood his ground that day in serenity and confidence; he won! And the outcome of that dramatic event was to shape Israel and help establish monotheism for all time to come.

Elijah never showed more courage than on Mount Carmel against those awesome adversaries, unless it was in his last hours when he tried to send away his beloved disciple Elisha and go out to meet death alone. Many persons, when they realize the impingement of the Mystery is near, beg others to stay close by. Elisha did see his mentor caught up into the heavens, but Elijah was not clingingly dependent on this one. He couragously faced the last step of transition, as he had all the crises that make up his history.

First of all, then, Elijah was remarkable for his courage,

and we should mark this well, for when it comes to the living of our days and nights, I know of no quality that is of more practical significance. George Buttrick has pointed out that life is more a succession of challenges than an intellectual riddle. And for that reason, one measure of courage is more helpful than ten abstract platitudes. Courage is the quality that brings every other virtue to its highest expression; for example, love given in the face of threat is always love at its best. Thus, we have a real model to emulate as again and again we witness the courage with which Elijah thrust himself into threatening situations.

But Elijah was also remarkable because of his profound insight into what was going on about him in history. It is in this sense that he qualifies for the title "prophet." Prophecy is not so much the ability to see into the future as it is the power to see deeply into present reality. A prophet is the one who discerns most profoundly what is going on now and where all this will lead. For a person with this gift, foresight is an outgrowth of insight, and this was exactly the case with Elijah; he "saw through" the people of his day with eyes like a spiritual x-ray.

Elijah realized the problem in Israel was that people were trying to live by two contradictory sets of ideals at the same time. In his graphic way, Elijah described this as "limping with two different opinions," or, translated more literally, "hopping first on one foot and then on the other." The whole nation, all the way up to the king himself, was being torn in two by this spiritual schizophrenia. You see, Ahab was a Hebrew by heritage and continued to adhere to the religion of Yahweh, even naming his sons in this tradition. However, Ahab had married a powerful Phoenician princess named Jezebel, who was an ardent worshiper of Baal, and she had been allowed to bring her religion into the country as well.

Elijah realized that a person can simultaneously embrace two mutually exclusive ideals about as easily as he can ride two horses in opposite directions at once. Personality is so made that it cannot tolerate such discord. As Jesus said, "No one can serve two masters: for either he will hate the one and love the other, or he will be devoted to the one and despise the other" (Matt. 6:24). The embracing of opposites is ultimately impossible and destructive. That is exactly what Elijah realized nine centuries before Christ, and that is why he spoke to the people on Mount Carmel with words to this effect: "You have to decide. If Yahweh is God, serve him. If Baal is God, serve him. But for heaven's sake, give up the notion that you can serve both at the same time. It simply cannot be done. The longer you try to embrace contradictions, the more divided you will become" (1 Kings 18:21, paraphrased).

Interestingly enough, Elijah's challenge is as relevant to us today as it was to those Israelites in the ninth century B.C. The names are different, but the essence of the choice between Baalism and Yahwehism is very much present in our own religious situation just now.

To understand what I mean by that statement, we need to look a little more closely at the nature of Jezebel's religion. Baalism was a fairly characteristic form of the kind of primitive religion found all over the Near East at the time. Its spirit was one of resignation to things as one found them and the attempt to survive as best one could. It saw life as fundamentally circular in nature—the cycle of the seasons and the stages of life going around and around without really getting anywhere. Therefore, the main goal of such religion was security and comfort. Placating the gods and "just getting by" were the overall aims.

Over against this, in stark contrast, stood the religion of Yahweh. Here was a religion of challenge. Growing, maturing, fulfilling—these were the ideals that began to break in with Abraham. There was something out ahead to strive for. History was seen as linear rather than circular. The flow of events was conceived as purposeful; that is, history was going somewhere. And God was seen as standing out ahead, beckoning human beings to become what they were not yet but could become.

Now, obviously, both of these religious systems cannot be right; by their very natures, they exclude each other. Then, as now, if we have as our primary goal a resignation to "things as they are," and if we see religion essentially in terms of comfort and security, then we cannot at the same time participate in the kind of experience that points toward climax and fulfillment. By the same token, putting our emphasis on challenge and promise will take its toll in terms of security and comfort.

Eventually we all have to choose to go one way or the other. And both in form and content, Elijah's insight is a challenge to our lives. Today we no longer think in terms of choosing between gods, but practically speaking there is still a lot of "limping with two different opinions." Sooner or later every one of us has to decide what kind of religion we are going to practice.

Comfort or challenge—which will it be? Will we settle into a state of cynicism and resignation, seeking only to make a better place for ourselves in the world as it is? Or will we dare to become adults and venture forth to make the world a better place—together with God to become creative change-agents? Will we resign ourselves passively to the goal of surviving with as little discomfort as possible? Or will we attempt to create something better, even at the cost of risk and suffering? These are the alternatives set before every individual and generation; it is to Elijah's credit that he realized this and called his contemporaries to decide in the face of it.

It is obvious, then, why our kinsman Elijah made such a vivid impression on the memory of Israel. He was a man of courage and insight who could both stand up to life and see deeply into life. And of course, he was a man of great faith, as his contest on Mount Carmel proved. However, to stop at this point would be to tell only part of the Elijah story. For alongside these obvious strengths, there were weaknesses as well, and the Bible, as always, is candid at this point. It makes no attempt to hide the fact that this same one who again and again manifested such great strength and courage also had his times of fear and cowardice and despair.

One of these times, in fact, occurred right after Elijah's stunning victory over the priests of Baal on Mount Carmel. As you may remember, after proving his point about who was God, Elijah personally killed all four hundred fifty prophets of Baal. When Queen Jezebel heard what had happened, she sent word to Elijah that within twenty-four hours she intended to do the same to him. And her threat frightened Elijah out of his wits! The Scripture simply says, "He was afraid, and he arose and went for his life" (1 Kings 19:3).

In fact, he did not stop running until he was clear out of the jurisdiction of Jezebel—way down to the south of Judea out in the desert.

This brave man, then, on occasion was capable of fear and cowardice. And the perceptive prophet who saw deeply into the nature of things and had such great faith in God also was capable of being blind to reality and of sinking into the depths of despondency and despair. For after all Elijah had done to stand up to the king and face down a whole army of prophets, it is amazing to read that this same one sat down one day under a broom tree and said, "I want to die. Lord, take away my life" (see 1 Kings 19:4). A few verses later we see him holed up in a cave, complaining to Yahweh, "All is lost; I'm the only one left who believes in you!" (see v. 10).

Here is a classic case of tension and exhaustion overwhelming a man until he became suicidal. Elijah lost all perspective on reality as the cloud of depression closed in on him. What a contrast is the Elijah of this moment with the heroic figure who had stood fearlessly before his adversaries with such confident trust in God.

Such a revelation about Elijah could lead to disillusionment if we approach life perfectionistically, but looked at from another perspective it offers hope, for it reminds us again that God's way of doing things is a process, not an instant completion. No person, not even a hero like Elijah, achieved greatness overnight or grew to wholeness immediately. The mixture of courage and cowardliness and insight and blindness and faith and despair that I experience in myself all the time is the usual way with us mortals. Even Elijah, who was strong at times, was not strong all the time, and God did not reject him because of this incompleteness. He patiently and mercifully worked with him, and that is good news for all of us!

Look, for example, at God's response to Elijah's suicidal depression. He did not condemn him for being a hypocrite or make him ashamed of having all those negative feelings. Rather, God proceeded to follow a very practical program of depression management. He began at the simplest level of Elijah's needs—the physical. Part of Elijah's spirit problem was undoubtedly due to the fact that he had been through a lot of stress and had been running in terror for a long distance. Thus, his body was depleted; it needed replenishment. So Yahweh provided rest and food. And things began to look very different to Elijah after a long night's sleep and a good square meal and time enough for "his soul to catch up with his body."

Having met Elijah's physical needs, the Lord then began to reorient Elijah's mind to reality, to show him that things were not nearly as bad as his fear and self-pity had led him to think. Yahweh took Elijah up on Mount Horeb (generally thought to be the same as Sinai, where once the commandments had been given to Moses), and reminded him that the ultimate redemptive instrument was not wind or fire or earthquake, but the "still, small voice" winning the affection of the individual heart.

You see, part of what had upset Elijah was probably his desire to find a shortcut for the work of redemption. He had expected the dramatic manifestation on Carmel to convert the whole world overnight, that is, to prove so overwhelmingly the existence of God that all humans would instantly believe. This is the temptation of all who confuse domination with devotion. You see, what God wants is a free response of love. He wants human beings to delight in him with all their hearts and minds and souls and strength, not just to be overwhelmed by his existence and cower in submission. And love like that does not come through a power transaction; it is the fruit of one-to-one wooing in which the affection of the heart is won.

In short, Elijah had to be reminded all over again of what God's work of redemption was all about: it is a process of devotion, not domination. And once he was able to accept that truth, the clouds of depression that had settled down so thickly over this man began to roll away.

Finally, Yahweh gave Elijah a new task to carry out and a gentle reminder that he was *not* the only possessor of truth left on the earth; there were seven thousand others who had not bowed their knees to Baal. It almost always helps a depressed person to realize that he or she is not alone, that there are others who care. And it helps to have work to do—a calling, a sense of purpose. Yahweh sent Elijah forth to anoint a new king of Israel and one of Syria—and also to anoint Elisha eventually to succeed him as prophet of the Lord.

And so Elijah was regiven the gift of life on the same terms as it had been given in the beginning—beyond his deserving, and through Yahweh's tender care. Thus, a despairing man was enabled to go back to face Queen Jezebel and the conflict of religions and the challenges of his own life with courage and insight once again.

How I hope every one of us can draw hope from this kinsperson of ours—from who he was and what happened to him. Emotionally speaking, this life of ours is a roller coaster, not an escalator. Like Elijah, we have our times of fullness and strength and faith, but also troughs of cowardliness and fear and depression. But the Good News is that God does not expect us to become complete overnight. First the seed, then the blade, then the flower—that is the Lord's way. Therefore, be of good courage, brothers and sisters of Elijah. This one had his great moments of courage and insight and faith; but he also had his times of failure and despair. And he was not abandoned. *He was not abandoned!* And neither will we be. It is God's hold on us, not our hold on Him, that is our hope. Let us then grow in that hope. Elijah overcame. So can we!

Questions for Thought and Discussion

1. Rethink the story of Elijah and identify the different forms of courage he demonstrated.

2. Can you think of persons today who are worthy of the title "prophet" because of their deep insight into the present and what this portends for the future?

3. What were some times in your life when you felt pulled between comfort and challenge—between resigning yourself to things as they are and striving to change things? In each instance, what was your decision? Would you decide differently today?

4. Describe the various forces that drained Elijah of his courage and drove him to the brink of despair.

5. How practical do you feel God's program of depression management is? What can it tell us about how we should respond to a friend who is suffering from depression?

13

AMOS
The Wages of Amnesia

THE KINSMAN WE COME NOW TO STUDY is one of the strangest figures of all the Old Testament. In the middle of the eighth century B.C., Amos suddenly appeared out of nowhere, uttered a word that was totally rejected at the time, and then just as swiftly disappeared back into oblivion and died.

However, to everyone's surprise, some twenty-five years later the brutal Assyrians overran the northern kingdom and took "the ten lost tribes of Israel" into captivity. The chosen people of God were shaken to their roots. How could such a thing happen to them? What about the promises of Yahweh that were supposed to be unshakable? In the confusion, someone remembered the words of the herdsman from Tekoa, which either he or someone else had written down. And when they read them again, they were amazed; for there, twenty-five years before, Amos had clearly foreseen this calamity and had boldly predicted that such a national collapse was on the way.

Why had they been so deaf? Amos's message had been the kind of unpleasant truth that is easier to deny than accept, but events now made such denial impossible. Belatedly, and somewhat sheepishly, the remnant of God's people began to take Amos's message seriously, and it has continued to illumine the human situation ever since.

The words of Amos were like the "time-released" capsules now on the market that spring into action sometime after they are taken. At the time he said them, they appeared to accomplish nothing; Amos was angrily ordered out of Bethel and told to go back to herding sheep. But years later the truth of what he had said became apparent. And his message proved to be a crucial factor in helping Israel deepen her understanding of the covenant and of what God really wanted for the chosen people. The prophet Amos was literally "a man ahead of his time," and that applies not just to the eighth century B.C. In many senses, he is still ahead of humankind, and has much to say to us that we would do well to heed.

Interestingly enough, the man Amos possessed none of the credentials that one would have expected for this kind of accomplishment. He was actually a desert shepherd, belonging neither to a family of prominence, nor to a circle of learning or any group of power-elite in Israel. He came from Tekoa, a desolate region south of Bethlehem near the Dead Sea, which to this day is a virtually uninhabitable waste of limestone hills. It was in this area, incidentally, that Bishop James Pike became lost several years ago and died of overexposure. If there ever was "a backside of nowhere," the region around Tekoa is it.

Although Amos lacked conventional credentials, he did have two distinct advantages that shaped him for his unique interpretive role. One was the fact that he and his family had lived in virtual isolation from the rest of Palestine during the five centuries that Israel had been there. This meant that they were uncontaminated by contacts with pagan religion. The covenant that Yahweh had made with his people at Sinai still burned purely in the consciousness of these simple folk. They had remained true to this distinctive vision rather than compromising with Canaanite religion, and this was the point of reference for Amos's insights. Once a year, it appears, he would journey to the cities of Jerusalem and Bethel and Samaria to sell his flocks, and he viewed what was going on much as Joshua and the early Israelites must have seen things when they came in fresh from the desert five hundred years before.

Coupled with this uncontaminated point of reference was a pair of eyes that were unusually observant. George Adams Smith has called the desert around Tekoa "a school of vigilance." Since there was really so little to see or hear in that sparse region, a shepherd learned to make note of every movement and sound and to ponder what it meant. This acute power of perception is one of Amos's most notable qualities, for it is evident from his writings that he did not miss a single detail as he traveled to and fro. As we would say today, "he took it all in," and this is what finally led him to explode in white-hot indignation. What he saw happening in eighth-century Israel did not square at all with what he had come to believe out of Sinai. It was this collision of past ideal and present reality that caused Amos to erupt like a smoldering volcano with words that live to this day because of their telling insight.

What did this herdsman see that so aroused him? In a word, he saw rampant inhumanity—human beings treating other human beings as if they were dogs or rocks. Amos could not believe the atmosphere of unfeeling brutality that pervaded that culture.

The root problem was an awesome gap between the rich and the poor that had been allowed to develop. Originally, there had been no class distinction among the Hebrews. They had all come from the very bottom of the social heap as slaves in Egypt, and for the first part of their life in the Promised Land, they had lived on equal footing in a kind of family-like mutuality. However, as always seems to happen when there is open opportunity, a few strong and aggressive families had begun to gain control of the main sources of wealth. Finally it had all become concentrated in a few hands, and those who had it proceeded to lose all sense of commonality with the rest of the nation. Instead of the growing wealth being used to enrich the quality of life in the whole society, it was diverted into useless and extravagant luxuries for the rich, who became obsessed with finding more and more elaborate and bizarre ways of amusing themselves.

Amos could hardly believe his eyes as he came in from the desert where everyone lived in a tent to see some people with not just one house, but two—one for the winter and one for the summer. He saw the rich lying around on couches of ivory inlaid with gold. He watched as they drank wine not by the glassful, but literally by the bucketful! He could not ignore the fact that the wealthy women had grown so fat with their indulgence that they reminded him of "the cows of Bashan."

All of this was taking place while the majority of the people did not even have enough to eat or a decent place to sleep. The poor were exploited and neglected, bought and sold "like a pair of sandals," and Amos was aghast at the spirit of inhumanity that characterized the society. The rich were "at ease in Zion" (Amos 6:1) and "not grieved over the ruin of Joseph" (v. 6).

What had happened to the fellow feelings that Israelites had had for Israelites in their earlier days? Where was the tenderness, the camaraderie, the sense of togetherness that had once made them a single family under God? Amos could find nothing now but hostility and destructiveness. The marketplace was an arena of dishonesty where all the scales were untrue and the government had become the arm of the privileged few. It was impossible for a poor man to get a fair judgment in any dispute. The judges could be bought for a few shekels of silver, and there was no compunction at all about buying and selling fellow Israelites into slavery.

No one in power seemed to have any concern at all about what was happening in the human dimension of society, and Amos could not contain himself any longer. Right in the middle of one of the high feast days in Bethel—a holiday like our Fourth of July—Amos stood up and began to roar like an angry lion in the name of the Lord. In words that literally dance up and down with white-hot vitality, he said two things to those startled people.

First of all, he said that in their present condition they had no future; they were sure to topple. Amos compared the nation to a bowl of overripe fruit that was about to be thrown out. He depicted God as standing in her midst with a plumb line like a builder, finding nothing that was put together securely enough to last. Israel had so defied the laws of corporate health that she was sick unto death.

This was not just the gloomy prediction of a chronic doom-sayer. This is an example of foresight growing out of insight. Amos saw deeply into the reality of the present situation and thus saw what was bound to result. He realized that injustice is a disease that wounds everybody in a society—the "haves" as well as the "have nots." When the masses are exploited and manipulated and dehumanized, such treatment drives them to bitterness and cynicism and makes them want to tear down the society rather than defend it. Author

James Baldwin once said that the most dangerous person in the world is the one who has nothing to lose. A person who has been excluded from any meaningful participation in a society and been given nothing but anguish and grief does not care if destruction comes to that society; in fact, that one will more than likely help bring such destruction about.

This is exactly what happened to Israel when the Assyrians attacked. The great host of the citizens were so beaten down that they had no reason to defend their country, and it collapsed before the invaders like a house of cards. By the same token, the rich people had so pampered themselves that they had grown weak and powerless. They had not done anything except amuse themselves for so long that they were flabby and unable to defend the country effectively.

This is exactly why unjust societies always eventually collapse. Since no one—neither the rich nor the poor—is participating healthily, there is no future for such an arrangement. Those who have strength have no reason to defend it, and those who have a reason to defend it have no strength.

John Woolman, a Quaker who lived before the Revolutionary War, said the same thing about slavery in this country. A full century before the Civil War, he realized that such an arrangement was destructive for everyone involved. It was bad not only for the slaves, who were robbed of their humanity and reduced to the status of mere property, but also for the slave owners, who did not develop as they should and became useless by totally relying on other people's labor.

The truth of Woolman's prediction struck home to me vividly, because I have heard again and again of how my great-grandfather on my mother's side lost his big plantation in Mississippi after the Civil War. He was used to dressing up and entertaining graciously and ordering others around, but when it came to being able to do any work himself, he was helpless. Thus, when the slaves on the place were freed, he could not do enough even to pay the taxes on the place, and he lost it all. In my great-grandfather's case, an unjust situation eventually took its toll on everyone; it dehumanized the slave and the slave owners in different ways.

This is precisely the kind of thing that Amos saw occurring in Israel; this was why he said, "You have no future." Such an arrangement of the frivolous rich and the embittered poor was sure to collapse—and it did, in fewer than twenty-five years. And does anyone today fail to realize that these words have a relevance for us? Injustice is not just an unfortunate condition; it is a fatal disease for any group of human beings. The sooner we realize this fact, the better.

But Amos went on to say a second thing to the people of Bethel. The reason they had no future, he told them, was that they had forgotten their past. Underneath all their social problems was a religious problem, and here is where the memory of the covenant at Sinai collided with their current religious practices.

One needs to realize that, before the advent of the religion of Yahweh, primitive men saw themselves as fundamentally worthless and felt that the gods couldn't care less about them. This meant that the main issue of religion was "How can we get the gods to love us? How can we alter the indifference—even the hostility—that exists in heaven for earth?" The answer that developed was an elaborate system of appeasing and ingratiating themselves with the gods. It was hoped that offering many gifts to the gods might effect a change of heart on the part of those deities.

Thus, all the primitive processes of ritual and sacrifice came into being. Sweet-smelling sacrifices were offered to heaven, the finest gifts that humans possessed were brought before the gods, and even the spectacle of human sacrifice was offered in the hope of amusing them. The way the prophets of Baal acted on Mount Carmel to get through to their distant deity is a vivid example of such an outlook. First they tried prayers, then sacrifices, and finally these prophets began to gash themselves in a desperate attempt to cause Baal to feel favorably disposed toward them.

It cannot be underlined too emphatically that the coming of Yahweh to Abraham represented an absolute break with this kind of religion. Here was a God who did not dwell in remoteness or indifference, but who of his own initiative moved closer to human beings with a desire to bless. Instead of demanding gifts from people, he wanted to give gifts to people! Here was the unbelievable spectacle of a God who was *for* human beings, whose greatest desire was that these individuals should come to the fullness of joy.

The God of Abraham was a deity whose greatest goal seemed to be the creation of a family of fully functioning human beings. The covenant that he made with Israel at Sinai is a perfect expression of this kind of concern. There is not one ceremonial requirement in the Ten Commandments. Every one of these laws is relational; that is, it shows how human beings can live so that their lives are made more full and whole. Stop for a moment and reflect: if the Ten Commandments were fully obeyed by every person, the result would be a humane society. There would be no killing, no stealing, no adultery, no lying, no envy. Rather, there would be the kind of mutual upbuilding that enables every human being to come to the fullness of what is in him or her and allows each to relate to all in ways that make for growth.

The covenant at Sinai was really a blueprint for genuine human fulfillment. It outlined how human beings are to relate healthily to God and to others and to themselves. And the point of all this is that biblical religion is a humanizing process. It points to a God who does not want a lot of things for himself, who desires most of all the development of his creatures. This means that we serve him best when we live humanely with ourselves and others.

What Amos realized was that after five hundred years of this covenant of blessing, Israel had fallen back into the religion of ritual and sacrifice! They had forgotten the God who had delivered them out of Egypt and wanted to bless them. Rather, they had lapsed back into pagan patterns of thinking, trying to please God by offering sacrifices and going through certain ceremonies. At the time Amos came to Bethel, he saw not only rampant inhumanity, but also bustling religious activity. However, this was ritualistic—not relational—religion. There were cereal offerings, burnt offerings, animal offerings, and all kinds of ornate ceremonies through which the priests led the people. But the old vision of *God for humankind* had been completely lost.

This is why Amos stood before the high temple and said, in the name of God: "I hate, I despise your feasts, and I take no delight in your solemn assemblies. Even though you offer me your burnt offerings and cereal offerings, I will not accept them, and the peace offerings of your fatted beasts

I will not look upon. Take away from me the noise of your songs; to the melody of your harps I will not listen. But let justice roll down like waters, and righteousness like an ever-flowing stream. Did you bring to me sacrifices and offerings the forty years in the wilderness, O house of Israel?"

The answer, of course, was no. What God desired was the humanization of man, not the ritualization of religion. To do justly, to love mercy, to walk humbly with him—this is what Yahweh wanted men and women to do. But Israel had forgotten this, which is why Amos spoke as he did. She had no future, for she had lost touch with her past. She had forgotten that divine favor does not have to be earned, but rather received and shared with other humans. The gift Yahweh wants from human beings is our help with his "pet project"—the fulfillment of the whole human family.

Why is this truth so hard for us to perceive? I guess it is because our self-hatred is so deep. We find it so hard to believe that we ourselves are loved and that other people have value in God's eyes. It comes so naturally to think of ourselves as worthless scum who have to try somehow to get God to love us, rather than to believe the incredible words of the gospel that he loves us already!

How hard it is to realize that God does not need anything for himself! He does not demand that we turn away from earth and give all of our affection to him. Rather, like the rich man who needs nothing for himself but has a special cause to which he is devoted, so God says to us, "You make me happiest when you give to my favorite charity—the human race."

Jesus grasped this point perfectly, for when he was asked to summarize the greatest of all the commandments, he said: "You shall love the Lord your God with all your heart, and with all your soul, and with all your mind . . . And a second is like it, You shall love your neighbor as yourself" (Matt. 22:37–39). Do you realize what this means? It means that the way we can best love God is by loving our neighbor.

This is the sacrifice that gives him delight, the gift that takes into account his desire. But this truth is so hard to grasp. I remember a church member who said to me angrily several years ago, "I get so tired of coming to church and hearing you talk about the human problems of the day—

poverty, peace, race, hatred. I come to church to forget all about these things. I come here wanting to think only of God and to focus my thoughts on his purity. I don't want to be reminded of people when I come to the house of God."

I understand this man's anguish, for he was expressing a feeling that is rooted deep in our consciousness and goes far back in our history. Human beings can be so despicable that our desire is to get as far away from them as we can. But I tried to remind him of what Amos was saying in his day—that such a movement is in direct opposition to the whole thrust of biblical faith. In the Bible God is always pictured as trying to get closer to humankind, not further away. The whole purpose of biblical religion is the humanization of the whole race. What God wants is a family of fully mature sons and daughters. And we serve him best by working with him toward that goal. In fact, Jesus told us how we can "kill two birds with one stone" in a religious sense. When we feed the hungry, clothe the naked, give drink to the thirsty— when we do any of this for the least of our brethren, we do something also for God! To be sure, God as person relishes the delight of our relating to him in gratitude and admiration, but we please him equally as much when we join him in his redemptive concern.

This is the vision Israel had forgotten. Her religion had lost touch with Sinai and lapsed back into paganism, and as always where there is no God like Yahweh, eventually there would be no humane humans. The inhumanity that leads to no future had developed in Israel through an amnesia to her past.

As I said earlier, no one paid any attention to Amos when he first offered these insights. But twenty-five years later, when the nation had collapsed and the unjust society had been overrun, they began to say, "Maybe Amos was saying something that we needed to hear after all." And his insights have not grown out-of-date even now. In fact, I wonder what that sharp-eyed herdsman would say about our country if he visited it today? And I wonder, would we be any more willing to hear him than the people of his day?

Questions for Thought and Discussion

1. Have you found that simplicity and scarcity does for you what it did for Amos, that is, make you more attentive and appreciative? Elaborate on your experience.

2. Whom does flagrant injustice hurt the most—the oppressed or the oppressors?

3. What are some specific ways Christians can work to fight injustice in our nation today?

4. Why do you think the Ten Commandments contain no ceremonial prescriptions?

5. How do we best show our true love for God?

14

HOSEA
The Courage of Compassion

"A PERSON WITHOUT A MEMORY is only half a person." "Amnesia is a sickness, not an asset." "An important part of coming to know who one is in the present is coming to terms with what one has been across the ages." You have encountered assertions like these again and again in these pages, inasmuch as they form the conceptual foundation of this book. I am working to help us understand who we are as the people of God by recalling the long memory of his people as recorded in the Old Testament. I want us to become aware of the kind of religious "blood" that is flowing in our veins and of those many realities that are at work in our religious heritage. This process can be an exciting pilgrimage to greater self-discovery. And now I invite you to move with me yet another step deeper into the immensity that lies behind us all.

Two of the ancestors we have just studied were men of raw and singular courage. Both Elijah and Amos were the kind of individuals who could stand up to hostile kings and priests and tell them what they did not want to hear, and this calls for a lot of bravery. However, our kinsperson in this chapter was equally as heroic a figure, although the form his courage took is altogether different from that of Elijah or Amos. His was the courage of compassion, of mercy, of tenderness. His coping was not with a hostile adversary, but with personal tragedy of the most intimate sort. But, let me not get ahead of the story here. Let me introduce you to the person himself; then we can live into what happened to him—and into what he did in response.

His name is Hosea. He lived in the northern part of Israel,
called Samaria, during the last half of the eighth century
B.C. He came just a little later in history than Amos, and
he was called on to live through the chaos that the herdsman
from Tekoa had seen coming upon the nation Israel. After
the death of King Jeroboam II, things had fallen apart in
the northern kingdom; one weak king after another tried
to rule, while the morale of the nation dwindled to nothing.
However, these national conditions were not the primary
forces bearing down on Hosea. It was something much closer
to home—or, to be more exact, it was the situation *in his
home*—that proved to be decisive for his life and ministry.

The references at this point are not completely clear; however, most scholars agree that this is what happened: Hosea
married a woman named Gomer, who at the time was pure
and chaste. All went well in the marriage through the birth
of their first child, a son whom they named Jezreel. Right
after this, however, the first hint of a shadow begins to appear
in Hosea's story. For when the second child—a girl—was
born, Hosea enigmatically named her Loruhamah, or as Brit-
ish Old Testament scholar George Adam Smith translates,
"She-that-never-knew-a-father's-love" (1:6). By the time a
third child came, the bitter truth was obvious; Hosea named
his new son Loammi—"Not-my-people" or "No-kin-of-
mine." Shortly after that the whole family structure collapsed,
and Gomer left home to go after the lovers who promised
her what she wanted.

There is no way to describe fully the anguish Hosea must
have felt at this turn of events. He was by nature a sensitive
and tender man, but even if he had not been, this sort of
experience would have been shattering. Try to put yourself
in his place. Here he was—disappointed as a husband, rejected as a man, alone, humiliated in the eyes of the community, and left with the care of three little children, two of
whom were not even his own. Lesser human beings would
have utterly crumbled under this kind of avalanche, and it
is to Hosea's credit that he was able to survive at all and
to keep going, which he did. However, he did much more
than that. He grappled with this most intimate of heartaches
as courageously as Elijah had grappled with the prophets
of Baal or Amos the wealthy citizens of Bethel. And out of

this grappling certain insights emerged—insights that represent permanent advances in the understanding of God and humankind in the drama of history.

Let me be specific about three of the truths that flowed from the wounds of this our kinsperson Hosea. The first has to do with the way God really feels about us humans and wants to be related to us. It could be that this insight came as something of a surprise even to Hosea. Because he was religious by inclination, it is not surprising that his personal tragedy drove him to the ultimate refuge and strength of the Holy One. And there, as he poured out his soul in anguish, he felt himself enveloped by a great Sympathy. It began to dawn on Hosea that Yahweh understood exactly what he was experiencing—because the Lord had been through the same trauma!

It was then that Hosea saw the tragic parallel between what Israel had done to Yahweh and what Gomer had done to him. We have no way of knowing just how Hosea had regarded the history of Israel up to this time, but out of the agony of his own betrayal he begins to employ the image of romance to describe the linkage between the Divine One and humanity: "Yahweh loves Israel the way I loved Gomer; therefore, look what our nation's sin has done to him!"

For that day, this was a shocking way of depicting the divine-human relationship, but it is true to the biblical story up to then. Yahweh's experience with Israel did have all the marks of a romance about it, beginning with the sheer mystery of his coming to her in Egypt. Why had Yahweh picked Israel and not the mighty Assyrians or the artistic Egyptians or the energetic Phoenicians to be his special beloved? It could no more be explained rationally than any two people can tell why they fell in love. And had not Yahweh brought Israel up out of bondage, wooed her in the desert, made Israel his "waif-bride" there at Sinai, and then set her up in the new home he had promised her from the beginning?

There is really no better analogy for describing God's feelings for humanity than this image of romance, yet few are those who have been able to grasp this or dare to believe it. That God really has passion for us, that he wants to be close to us and to share affection with us in a relationship of deepest intimacy, that we and our companionship really matter to God—such thoughts are miles beyond the way most of us usually think about the Holy One. At best, if we think of our relationship with him at all, it is in terms of fear or remoteness, the relationship being a legal or a casual one. But a romantic relationship—God's loving me as a lover loves his beloved—that is an image which catches many of us by surprise.

But, let me repeat: here is one of the deepest truths of the biblical revelation! After all, what did Jesus say was the first and greatest of all the commandments? It is not "You shall *respect* the Lord your God" or even *"serve* your God." It is rather: "You shall *love* the Lord your God with all your being." And how is this possible? We love him because he first loved us! This is the model biblical religion always sets at the heart of divine-human relations; and the greatness of someone like Francis of Assissi lies in the fact that he recognized this fact and lived out of it. G. K. Chesterton once wrote that the only way to understand Francis and the wild things he did religiously was to recognize him for what he was—a lover of God, as passionate and ecstatic as any troubadour was for his lady. Hosea was one of the first to grasp this insight: that the way of God with humankind and, hopefully, of humankind back to God is the way of romance—a relation of love and affection and mutual intimacy.

If this image ever breaks through to us, it can utterly transform the way we feel toward God and self and other humans and the whole world. It can also shed light on the real nature of sin as much more than violating a taboo or breaking a cosmic law. For Hosea's vision of the relationship between God and humankind is that at bottom sin means violating a gracious trust—breaking faith with the one who loves us the way Gomer broke faith with Hosea.

Herein is a place where Hosea's approach differed from that of Amos. For all of his courage and perception, the only emotion the shepherd from Tekoa showed was that of intense anger. Israel had broken the laws of nature and was going to have to pay for it, according to Amos, and little sadness was registered over the state of affairs. Hosea realized the same thing, but he also saw that sin breaks more than laws—it breaks hearts as well. And after Hosea, neither God nor sin could ever be regarded impersonally again. By realizing that the Almighty felt toward Israel and all humankind the way he felt for Gomer and therefore was affected by the sin of Israel the way he had been affected by Gomer's sin, Hosea immeasurably deepened and personalized the image of God, and the emotional stakes of the divine-human encounter were raised forever.

A second insight that grew out of Hosea's tragedy had to do with the relation of knowledge or the lack of it to human sinfulness. Hosea was forced to plumb "the mystery of iniquity," to ponder *why* Gomer would do what she did in leaving a good husband and a family for the life of a prostitute, or, at a deeper level, why Israel would desert her husband, Yahweh, to go "awhoring after their idols" (Ezek. 6:9). The answer Hosea came to is the same that Jesus articulated from the cross when he prayed, "Father, forgive them; for they know not what they do." This means that the problem lies in profound ignorance or lack of knowledge as to where the real good is to be found.

All humans are alike in wanting to fulfill their natures and to do those things that will result in joy. The difficulty, however, is one of means; that is, of not really knowing how to accomplish these positive goals. For example, Gomer undoubtedly thought that leaving home and following her lovers held more promise for joy than staying with Hosea, and that failure of judgment—that ignorance, her lack of knowledge— was her undoing.

Harry Emerson Fosdick once preached a famous sermon about a man in New York who wanted to go to Detroit. This man bought a ticket and boarded a bus and rode for fourteen hours. When he got off, however, he discovered he was in Kansas City, not Detroit. For all his good intentions and efforts, he had not arrived where he wanted to be, for the simple reason that he had gotten on the wrong bus! His means were imperfect; they did not correspond to his ends. This was Gomer's problem, Israel's problem—the problem of all us sinful folk. Our intention is a proper one—we want to fulfill ourselves and to know joy. The problem lies in knowing how to do this! We do not know the things that make for our peace, as Jesus once put it (Luke 19:42), and so we perish for the lack of pragmatic knowledge about what really works for our own good.

This is a theme Hosea underlines again and again in his book, blaming prophets and priests alike for not learning what God has been trying to teach them from the first. Had Gomer only realized what Hosea was like, she would never have left. She did come to realize this later, after being manipulated and maltreated again and again by her lovers. But just as in the case of the prodigal son, it took a lot of suffering in "the far country" to open her eyes to what she could have known from the start, if only she would have learned.

One of our most basic human problems is our profound ignorance of God and life. Jesus summed it up by saying: "They know not him that sent me" (John 15:21), and he indicated that this is why we suffer as we do. Jesus also said, to the woman at the well, "If you only knew who was talking to you, you would ask him for everlasting life" (John 4:10). But this is where our problem lies; we refuse to be taught about who God really is. And yet the Holy One continues in his efforts to enlighten us. He came among us in Israel; he sent his son to show us the Father; and to as many as receive him he still gives power to become children of God, that is, to be delivered from the ignorance of our sin (see John 1:12). Hosea put his finger on the problem when he said that at the bottom of our sinfulness was a matter of ignorance.

The last insight that came to Hosea, however, is perhaps the most moving of all, for in his sharing with God and in the identity of agony he had come to feel with him, Hosea caught a glimpse into the Holy One's deepest nature and into how that One was responding to Israel's infidelity. In what has to be the most plaintive section of the whole Book, Yahweh is overheard as saying, "How can I give you up, O Ephraim! How can I hand you over, O Israel! . . . My heart recoils within me, my compassion grows warm and tender. I will not execute my fierce anger, I will not again destroy Ephraim; for I am God and not man, the Holy One in your midst, and I will not come to destroy" (11:8–9).

Such a reaction is hard to take in at first, for it avoids both of the extremes deep emotion might be expected to take. One approach would be to refuse to take the issue of sin seriously and to evade the accompanying agony by retreating into superficiality. The other extreme would be to take the problem to its logical conclusion and to explode in destructive anger against one who appears to be hopeless. Hosea depicts Yahweh's response to Israel as being neither of these. He does not gloss over the issue casually, for unfaithfulness is a serious matter and Israel must learn by her own suffering what it was she had done. There will be calamity and defeat and exile, Hosea sees, but that is not all. Yahweh still loves Israel, even though she has not loved him, and out there in the desert of exile the Holy One vows to woo her once again, to try to win her affection. There is hope in the heart of the Aggrieved that Israel can be restored and become a faithful lover once again.

This has to be the best Good News ever heard on earth—that God is like this, that "while we are yet sinners" and continue to be sinners, he still loves us and is willing to work with us in building a relationship. Let me remind you that he does not have to be that way. There is nothing in us or the universe that decrees that the Everlasting One has to be merciful or that mercy has to be everlasting. That he is this way is a sheer and joyous miracle which we cannot explain but can only celebrate. What Hosea overheard in the heart of the Most High came to its clearest expression on the cross and in the resurrection of Christ, where the Lover whom we had forsaken proved that he would not forsake us.

The story of Hosea however, ends not just with insight—as powerful as it is—but with imitation. It appears that Hosea was not altogether astonished to find that Yahweh had not given up on Israel, for he too was made in the image of such a God, and evidence of Yahweh's steadfast love lay in the fact that he still loved Gomer and had hope for her! She had broken his heart, but not the bond of his affection. Thus, when he saw her reduced to slavery—probably having sold her body so often that she had nothing left to sell but herself—he did not reproach her and say bitterly, as Amos might have done: "It serves you right. You humiliated me and made me suffer. Now it's your turn to be humiliated and to taste some of your own medicine."

No, without a word, Hosea went and got fifteen shekels of silver and a homer and a half of barley—a slave's ransom. Laying it at the feet of the slave trader, he pointed to Gomer and said, "I want her." It was Hosea's way of identifying with the God who had identified with him, of beginning the painful task of trying to rebuild what had been torn down.

We are not told in the Book how Gomer responded to Hosea's proposal. From one standpoint, it is almost unthinkable that she could have refused such an offer of incredible mercy. Surely, if anything could get through to a human heart and change it, an act such as this would do it. For Hosea to do this for her, in light of what she had done to him, what could be more compelling?

However, perhaps the issue is left open for a reason—to underline the fact that, for all its power, love is not absolute. By its very nature, it will not coerce or force. And that is the final terror of life. God is love, not just power, which means he will not bludgeon us into the kingdom against our will. He will woo us, persuade us, forgive us, do all that can be done to manifest his love, but the response is ultimately left up to us. If we will not accept his love, he will take our no for an answer—and that is why there is a hell. It is not a monument to God's wrath, mind you, but a monument to his love, to the fact he will let us stay out in the darkness forever rather than force us into the light.

We do not know, then, what Gomer did, but that really is not the most important question now. The burning issue is that God loves you more passionately than any human ever loved another human, and even though you have sinned against him, he will forgive and wants to share his love with you again. What will you do about that? This is the issue our kinsman, Hosea, poses before us. Let's forget about Gomer, then, and face the real question: How will we respond to the God who says, "I made you and I love you, and now I have bought you—will you share life with me forever?"

Questions for Thought and Discussion

1. How do you feel about using the image of romance to describe God's relation to us and our relationship to him?

2. To what degree have you found that ignorance is a big part of sinful actions? Do you feel taking this view "lets off" the sinner too easily?

3. What do you think about the assertion that the reality of hell has more to do with the nature of love than the nature of wrath?

4. From Hosea's insight, is there an unforgiveable sin? If so, what is it?

15

ISAIAH
Saying Yes to the Real You

IN THIS PROCESS of "thumbing through" our family album
called the Old Testament and getting reacquainted with some
of our most important religious ancestors, one thing has become very obvious—that our heritage is varied and diverse!
It must "take all kinds" to make up the people of God, for
that is exactly what we encounter when we begin to remember
who we are.

For example, among the biblical forebears we have re-
viewed in this book, two were very poor and from nondescript
families—Elijah a penniless sojourner and Amos a desert
herdsman. However, the kinsman we come to focus on now
was the very opposite—an aristocrat of the highest order.
The whole life of the prophet Isaiah was spent within the
urban confines of Jerusalem, where he was steeped in the
finest culture of his day. He was also well connected on the
highest levels. For a period of over forty years, and through
the reign of four different kings, he had easy access to the
palace and was sought out often by the rulers for his counsel.

Isaiah was one of those rare individuals who seem to be
gifted in all areas. He was at once a person of words *and* a
person of action. He had poetic gifts of the highest magnitude
that enabled him to see into matters with great penetration.
And surprisingly enough, this poet was also politically astute;
that is, he was just as shrewd a judge of kingdoms like Assyria
or Egypt as he was of figures of speech. Because of his fantastic endowments and dedication, George Adam Smith calls
him "easily the greatest man of his day." He was to eighth-
century Judah something of what Winston Churchill was to

England in the 1940s, and for this reason we have cause to look closely at his life and see what we can learn from him. Here is a kinsperson of whom we can really be proud. Let us approach him in such a way that we can profit from him as well.

The book that bears Isaiah's name is the longest of any of the prophetic documents in the Old Testament, but it is now clearly recognized that only the first thirty-nine chapters pertain to the man who lived from 760 B.C. to around 700 B.C. Some hundred and fifty years later, a "second Isaiah" arose after the Exile to interpret that experience for Israel, and his words were linked to the words of his spiritual predecessor. The Isaiah we are concerned about here lived during the same era as Amos and Hosea and shared much of their outlook about the nature of things.

Isaiah was just as indignant as Amos about the way Israel had missed the genius of her religion. It was not smoky sacrifice or elaborate ritual that Yahweh wanted from his people; it was love and compassion and justice for their fellow human beings. The building of a human community was the passion of Yahweh, not the building of temples and altars. But Israel had forgotten this and lapsed back into the manipulations of paganism. And because little attention was being paid to the plight of the people, the social fabric in Israel had become rotted with injustice and was sure to collapse.

Variations of this theme appear again and again throughout Isaiah and reflect his commonality with the other eighth-century prophets. However, I want to focus our attention now on two other aspects of Isaiah's thought, areas where he broke new ground and thus carries us beyond Elijah and Amos and Hosea in spiritual understanding. What I want to underline is Isaiah's concept of God and of what doing God's will is like.

First of all, Isaiah has much to teach all of us about the mysterious reality of God and about how this One is to be regarded. We saw in the previous chapter how a personal experience like Hosea's could affect a person's whole outlook. The same thing could be said of Isaiah, for something happened to him as a young man that left an indelible mark upon him. Interestingly enough, Isaiah's was also an experience of shattering disillusionment—not with his wife, but with a king whom he had idolized as a boy. This king's name was Uzziah, and he was widely recognized as being the most effective ruler over Judah since the time of Solomon. For forty years he had guided the affairs of this little state with great wisdom and stability, and prosperity had come to his people because of him. Naturally, he was admired, especially by impressionable youths such as Isaiah.

However, toward the end of his reign, Uzziah had done an impulsive thing. One day in the temple he had become impatient about the way the incenses were being offered, had arrogantly gotten up and pushed aside the appointed priests, and with his own unordained hands had offered the sacrifice. In that culture, this was an act of blasphemous over-reaching even for a king. And before Uzziah had left the temple, blotches of white had began to show on his face and hands—a sign of the onset of leprosy. Uzziah's affliction had been widely interpreted as God's judgment on his pride, and the king who had once been loved so dearly had been relegated to a leper cottage, where he died not long there-after.

This event shook the young Isaiah down to his toes. That his hero would do such a thing and then be so swiftly judged set Isaiah wondering, "Just who is this God, Yahweh, anyway? What kind of Power are we up against?"

Now, we need to realize at this point that Israel had fallen into that kind of carelessness—what even might be called a "coziness"—with the Divine One that is always a sign of deca-dence. They had reiterated so often to themselves that they were "the chosen people," "the beloved of Yahweh," that they had begun to presume on this One and to treat him lightly. Uzziah's sin was reflective of the attitude of the whole nation, which is why what happened to him startled everyone so. Suddenly, it became apparent that this Yahweh was no casual Plaything. He was more like fire or lightning—an awe-some Force that needed to be treated with respect. A new note of seriousness was injected into religion because of what happened to the king, and Isaiah for one began to ponder "the God-question" with a fresh sense of fear and trembling.

Then, one day in the Temple, perhaps on the very site where his idol had sinned and fallen, something happened to Isaiah that was to change his life forever. In a word, *God* happened to him, overwhelmed him, encountered him as only the Almighty can encounter one, and he "saw" as he had never seen before a vision of what God was like—his holiness, his vastness, his mercy. Out of this experience, Isaiah began to speak of God as "the Holy One of Israel." This is what the seraphim had chanted: "Holy, holy, holy is the Lord of hosts," and this is the first thing any one of us needs to understand about the Ultimate One.

The word *holy* has come to mean something in our language that is different from its original connotation. We tend to equate it with something moral or ethical; however, it originally meant "to be separate" and referred to the uniqueness, the distinctness, the one-of-a-kind-ness of a person or object. To call God "holy" meant that he was utterly different from anything else, and this is the truth that needs to be the beginning point of all our reflections about him.

We have learned on lower levels to make distinctions in the way we relate to other beings. For example, I relate in one way to an animal, in another way to myself, and in yet another to other people—be they family, friends, or foes. In a word, I am capable of many forms of relationships to the various aspects of reality, yet none of these is quite identical to my relation to God. In every one of these cases, I am relating to something that is created just as I am, something that has its existence because Another wills it to rise into existence out of nothing. With God, however, the relation is unique, for this One is the Source of all. This One has life in himself and is dependent on nothing else. As a result, there is no real analogy for this relationship—my linkage with God stands apart as utterly unique and distinct.

Realizing this can save an individual from confusion and error. I am always hearing people say, "How do I know there is a God? I've never seen him. He has never spoken to me." And the problem is that they expect God to become an Object alongside other objects and to relate to him the way we relate to all other creatures. But this is never the case, for God is radically different from everything else—he is the Source of life, not one of life's creations. This means we can expect his dealings with us to be unique. They will have a certain "ring" to them that is unlike any other experience we have ever had, yet somehow we will know, as Isaiah did, that this is God, the Holy One, revealing himself in his own way.

The problem here is that we set up criteria of expectation

on our own. In other words, we decide in advance what an experience with God must or must not be, using as criteria the experiences we have had with other creations. How, then, can the utterly unique One ever get through to us? What we must have is radical openness, a willingness to let this One assume whatever shape he will and to trust that he can make himself known without analogy.

This does not mean that an encounter with God will not bear some resemblance to other experiences; after all, there in the temple Isaiah spoke of "seeing" and "hearing" and "feeling" God's mystery. But Yahweh's authenticating thrust was more than any one of these sensory experiences. Isaiah was encountered by the Holy One himself and *he knew it,* and while God used many of Isaiah's senses to reveal himself, the whole revelation was more than simply the sum of the parts.

Perhaps one of the best ways to illustrate this point is to compare truth to fact. My commitment to truth as a way of life is something very different than my relation to a single fact. The second is rooted in the first and an expression of it, but truth is deeper and more inclusive than any fact or collection of facts. So it is with God as the Holy One. He is the Ground of all being, the ultimate Source of all; therefore, there is nothing with which to compare him—there are no other realities like him.

Isaiah sensed this fact in his encounter in the temple, and it is the beginning step of wisdom concerning God. He is literally the Holy One—totally incomparable. Thus, we must let God be God, and let him come to us as he will. To demand in advance that he be this or that is to miss him, for he will always come as Surprise. How else can the Uncreated One be in the midst of creation?

From this beginning point of holiness, Isaiah moved on to recognize the vastness of God. He is greater than any human could dare imagine in both an extensive and an intensive sense. You can get some sense of what I am talking about by looking through either a telescope or a microscope. Both instruments show that there is more to the universe than meets the naked eye. A telescope enables us to see a vastness beyond the reach of our farthest sight, while a microscope enables us to see a minuteness of detail that is beneath our natural powers of penetration. Isaiah learned that the same thing could be said of God—that he is bigger than Israel had imagined him, but also nearer.

Isaiah depicts Yahweh not only as high and lifted up in heaven, but also as the Ruler of all the nations. This insight represented a new horizon for Hebrew thought. Up to this time, Israel had tended to confine its concept of God to Palestine and its surroundings, but Isaiah exploded that parochialism. He saw the whole earth as belonging to God and controlled by him—he even saw mighty Assyria and Egypt as "rods in Yahweh's hands." Thus the distinction between God's "agents" and "instruments" arose. Israel was to be "an agent," in that God had revealed to her his purpose and invited her to cooperate knowingly. A power like Assyria, however, was still only an "instrument"—used by God but largely unconscious of what was taking place.

God, then, according to Isaiah, is vaster than anyone had ever dreamed. At the same time, he is nearer, in that he is concerned about every detail of life on earth, down to how the women dressed and what happened to the lowliest widow and orphan. This came very clear to Isaiah—that everything matters to Yahweh. And holding onto this paradox is the second step of wisdom as far as understanding God's mystery is concerned. Our tendency is to embrace only one side of this polarity or the other—either to make God so high and vast that he is remote and aloof, or to bring him so close that he becomes a cozy chum and not the Lord of all the universe. To embrace at one and the same time the telescopic and microscopic dimensions of God's reality is true to the biblical vision, and for this insight, along with the sense of what it means to be holy, we are indebted to our kinsperson Isaiah.

The other important truth to be learned from Isaiah has to do with the way he understood himself in relation to the purpose of God. Out of his encounter with God in the temple, Isaiah sensed a positive identification with what God was doing in the world. And after being mercifully purified, he willingly volunteered to collaborate with what God was doing. When the question went out: "Whom shall I send, and who will go for us?" Isaiah answered, "Here am I! Send me" (Isa. 6:8).

The important point here is that Isaiah saw obedience to God as a way of self-realization, not a way of self-denial. In his thinking, the doing of God's will was the completion of creation rather than a negation of it.

I have a minister friend who insists that for a call of God to be authentic, it must be a conscription. "No man should volunteer for God's service," he claims. "He must be drafted, apprehended, dragged in kicking and screaming against his will." I have argued with him at this point, partially on the basis of Isaiah's experience, and suggested that such a position is on shaky ground theologically because it separates the God who creates from the God who calls. If they are one and the same, as I believe they are, then what sense would it make for the gifts of creation to be ignored and a person to be called to do what he or she despises? I am convinced that obedience to God is basically a way of self-fulfillment, not a way of self-denial.

How, then, does this square with Jesus' famous words about a disciple's needing "to deny himself and take up his cross" (Matt. 16:24; Mark 8:34; Luke 9:23)? This is a point that needs to be cleared up once and for all, and the key to it is distinguishing between the true self which God created and the fantasy self each one of us creates on our own in preference to God's gift.

I have said many times before that I see self-hatred as the root of all sin. According to Genesis, this was the problem of the first human beings in the Garden. They were given a beautiful life—individual selves, a world, a purpose—and then a snake came along and upset the whole thing. How? By appealing to Adam and Eve's dissatisfaction with the selves they had been given in creation. "You could become like God," the serpent whispered, "something different than the lousy self you are." And Adam and Eve fell for the serpent's line. However, this would never have happened had they accepted from the first the fact that the selfhood they had been given by God was tremendously good. It was out of dissatisfaction with "the God-given self" that sin entered history and the great distortion of creatures trying to be creators began.

The nation Israel made this same mistake. God created them to be a special kind of people, to show the world how a community could work in which human beings knew they were loved and therefore could love each other. They were to point the way beyond the conflict and domination that had characterized all societies up to that time, to be a means by which all the families of the earth could learn to bless themselves. But no, like Adam, they despised that selfhood in favor of trying to be political and domineering like all the other nations. Isaiah saw this fact clearly, and this is why he counseled every king for forty years against getting entangled in foreign alliances. Being a political power was not Israel's calling—hers was a humanizing vocation—but she could not accept that, and opted for creating her own selfhood over against the identity God had given her.

This is not just Adam's and Israel's problem; it is everyone's problem—mine and yours as well. This insight connects up directly with some of my earliest childhood experiences. I well remember at age five wanting to be tall and thin and have straight black hair and be named Dick. All of this, you realize, was very different from the personhood I had been given. I remember going to a church camp in North Carolina the summer before my senior year in high school and meeting a girl from another state, whom I dated for those six days. I had never seen this girl before and never expected to see her again, so I proceeded to feed her the biggest "line" about myself you can imagine. I claimed I had been an All-City halfback in football the year before, that my father was president of an insurance company, that we had two Cadillacs, that I had been to Europe three times, and that I could have gone back that summer except that I had chosen to go to church camp instead!

Now, before you judge me too harshly for my behavior, let me say that some of the things she told me about herself were equally as outlandish. But, setting aside for the time being the question of truthfulness, the significant thing to me about this whole exchange was how little I liked or accepted the real John Claypool, and how utterly given I was to fantasy. The John Claypool I dreamed up to present to this girl was obviously who I wanted to be in preference to what God had made me to be.

I am convinced that this kind of fantasy self is the self Jesus calls us to deny if we would become his disciples. We are to say no to the self we created out of dissatisfaction with the gift of God, and thus by a double negative get back to the positive. To deny my fantasy self is a way of saying yes to my real self, and this is what obedience to God is all about. The fact that doing this may feel like being drafted or saying no to all our desires grows out of what we have been doing so long to the gift of God within us. However, at bottom, the way of obedience is a positive one and the way to true self-fulfillment, for saying yes to God is never done at the expense of one's real self—only the unreal one. And the quicker I begin to love what God loves—namely, the real John Claypool, the person he has made—the sooner I am on the way to joy.

The life of Isaiah is a living testimony to this way of seeing self. If ever there was a secure, "together," effective human being, it was this prophet. He had about him the air of true authority, no matter what the circumstances. And this grew out of his having accepted the gift of his personhood and then saying to God, "I want to obey. In your will is my fulfillment. I volunteer to become that good thing you made me to be. I accept Isaiah."

Would to God, the Holy One of Israel, that every one of us could do the same thing! If that could happen, then it would not just be a matter of our being proud to have Isaiah in our family tree. Then Isaiah could be proud of us, for we would have joined him in the great secret of joy.

Questions for Thought and Discussion

1. What do you think about the idea that God is unlike any thing else in all creation? What does that suggest about our experiences with him?

2. Which aspect of God is the hardest for you to accept—his telescopic vastness or microscopic nearness?

3. How do self-denial and self-fulfillment relate to each other?

4. How well do you like the person God made you to be?

16

JEREMIAH
The Hope of Losing to God

THOMAS JEFFERSON WAS RIGHT, I believe, in declaring that "all men [persons] are created equal." In terms of our worth in the sight of God, every one of us stands on the same level. But this equality must not be confused with "just-alikeness," for in terms of temperament and gifts and the opportunities open to us in history, there are vast differences between individual persons.

No better illustration of this fact could be found anywhere than in comparing the ancestor we just discussed, the prophet Isaiah, with the man who is the focus of this chapter—Jeremiah. The Books bearing their names appear back to back in the Holy Scripture, but between them is not only a space of some one hundred years of history, but also a vast chasm of temperament and life experience. A few pages back, I depicted Isaiah as he really was in history—a princely, aristocratic sort of person who always seemed to be acting out of a stance of positive strength. He was wellborn and utterly secure, and thus could speak frankly and fearlessly to kings and common folk alike. There was an air of assurance and authority that characterized everything Isaiah said and did.

However, the prophet Jeremiah comes through the information we have about him as an entirely different sort of person. From start to finish, his life was torn apart by inner strife and uncertainty and ambiguity. If Isaiah's life experience could be likened to an escalator which rose steadily and progressively higher, Jeremiah's experience could be compared to a roller coaster—forever hurtling up and down. Nowhere in Scripture, except perhaps in a few selected

Psalms, do we witness quite the wild fluctuation of feelings as is found in Jeremiah's book.

Perhaps part of the reason for this is that we know more of Jeremiah's inner moods than we do of others'. His book represents a new form of prophetic record, for it contains not only his words to the people, but also his inner dialogues with God. However, significant as this factor may be, it cannot be used to account for the whole difference between Jeremiah and the rest of Scripture.

The fact needs to be faced squarely that Jeremiah's life was a battlefield of emotional conflict. He was capable of soaring in ecstasy as he delighted in God, yet he also knew times of horrible depression when he accused the Holy One of being unreliable and cursed the day he was born—even the man and the woman who had brought him into the world. He also could be unbelievably compassionate with other people, manifesting a tenderness of feeling that is rare indeed. Yet at other times he was just as extreme in his hostility and vindictiveness toward those who had failed him or hurt him. Jeremiah was not a plaster saint who was always strong and good, and for that very reason is worth our learning more about him.

To be perfectly honest, I can feel closer to this "up-and-downer" than to the aristocratic and controlled Isaiah. My emotional life is also more like a roller coaster than an escalator. My hour-to-hour experience has more struggle in it than an effortless unfolding from height to height, and unless I am badly mistaken, most of you join me in such an identification. There are just not many Isaiahs around in any age. But our brother Jeremiah, who found life difficult every inch of the way, is someone to whom we can feel close and, hopefully, one from whom we can learn a great deal.

The first thing I propose here is that we use "a zoom lens" on Jeremiah's experience, that is, move in closely and ask *why* his life was so conflictual and filled with such emotional extremes. When we do this, I think we will find two reasons that were foundational for his conflicts.

I believe one of the reasons for the conflict in Jeremiah's life is the self-concept out of which he proceeded to live his life. Unlike Isaiah, Jeremiah tended to be negative about himself. In the first glimpse we get of him in his Book—

the moment of his call—this tendency is very evident. God declared that before the foundations of the earth he had meant for Jeremiah to be his spokesperson in that era: before he was formed in the womb or born into history, Jeremiah had been consecrated for that purpose. But he had trouble accepting such an identity. The image he had of himself was much less than this, and this low self-image led him to demur by saying, "I can't do that; I do not know how to speak. I'm just a child, a weakling, a worthless nothing" (see Jer. 1:6).

From the very beginning, then, Jeremiah seems to have thought less of himself than he ought to have thought, and this inferiority complex, this sense of inadequacy, plagued him all through his life. He was never able to shake completely his self-despising, although God struggled with him patiently all through his days, and this has to be part of the explanation of why Jeremiah had such a hard time in his life. Isaiah was more fortunate in this regard. As we saw in the last chapter, he volunteered at the moment of his call and seemed to know how to claim the promise of his inheritance from the heavenly Creator. However, Jeremiah was not able to do this with any sense of assurance, which is one reason the lives of these two turned out to be so different.

From the evidence we have before us, it is impossible to pinpoint absolutely where Jeremiah's negative self-concept originated, but undoubtedly it began at home and was rooted in the way he was treated as a boy. He came from a priestly family who lived in a village northeast of Jerusalem, and we do know that later in his life some of his family turned against him and even joined in a plot to assassinate him. It could have been that Jeremiah's earliest childhood experiences were negative ones, so that from the beginning Jeremiah thought of himself as incapable of any task.

Dr. Haim Ginott has written extensively about how such a thing can happen to a child. In his view, there is nothing more damaging to a child's self-concept than sweeping "be-ing" statements like You are lazy"—or "sloppy," or "dumb," or "bad." A child experiences this sort of statement as a literal broadside to his or her whole personhood and may conclude that he or she is totally worthless, incapable of changing for the better. Dr. Ginott strongly urges that parents confine their negative statements to the "doing" level. For example, a parent can and ought to say to a child in relation to some specific act, "Look, you are doing this sloppily" or "You are acting dishonestly and this bothers me." We can thus focus on a specific problem without casting aspersions of the totality of the child's personhood. This is the same principle as in the well-known formula of "loving the sinner but hating the sin." To affirm a person at the being level and at the same time modify behavior at the doing level is the healthiest approach to relationships. But very possibly this was not the way Jeremiah was treated as a little child, and perhaps this is one reason why we see him as a young man shrinking back fearfully from the challenge of God's call.

However, to put all the blame on Jeremiah's parents for what they did or did not do would not be fair, for this spirit of self-despising many of us have is deeper and wider than the influence of the two people who birthed and raised us. It is a disease that seems to go all the way back to the beginning; I believe it is closely tied with what the theologians call "original sin." For reasons too deep and old for any of us to understand fully, we all seem to come into this world tainted with negative feelings about ourselves, and this has always been the ultimate battleground for God's grace.

Dr. Thomas Harris, the well-known author of *I'm OK— You're OK*, says that no matter how ideal the parent-child relationship, everyone still enters adolescence with abundant "I'm not OK" feelings, and this is where the work of God must take place—at the deepest level, where we fashion images of ourselves. What God is pictured as doing with Jeremiah in the outset of the Book is therefore what he has to do with each of us—to set the images he has of us over against the images we have developed of ourselves across the years.

The story of how Jeremiah came to be and what he was meant to become from God's perspective was so different from the record he had been playing to himself about himself that he could hardly believe it. But this is what I believe the story of Jeremiah is all about—how God struggled to change the record that was playing inside Jeremiah, how he mercifully and patiently retold Jeremiah's story to him until finally he became re-educated emotionally and learned to accept what God loved—his real self.

Such a process is always slow and painful, which is why Jeremiah was up and down so often, but I repeat: this is the basic work of grace. Our ultimate struggle with God is not just in terms of what we believe about him, but in terms of what he believes about us. Coming to accept and affirm this is no easy task for chronic lifelong self-haters like Jeremiah or you or me, but to use a hackneyed phrase, "this is where it's at" spiritually. And because God and Jeremiah started out worlds apart in terms of what they thought of Jeremiah, it took a lot of doing finally to get the two of them together.

The other reason for Jeremiah's agony has to be the particular time in which he was called to live. We need to remember that nations, just like persons, can get sick and waste away and finally die, and Jeremiah happened to be born in the era when Israel as a nation was terminally ill. His ministry can be dated from 626 B.C. until 587 B.C., when the Babylonians conquered Jerusalem and destroyed the temple and captured the king, which meant that David's throne was vacated forever. It was a horrible period for any child of Abraham to have to live through, and added to Jeremiah's problems was the fact that he saw what was coming before most other people did and advocated a stance of realistic acceptance. Such perception was ahead of its time and "against the grain," and almost everybody wound up hating Jeremiah for the position he took.

As in many cases of terminal illness, a great sense of unreality pervaded Jerusalem in Jeremiah's time. These people had not been true to the covenant of Yahweh. They had not done justly or loved mercy or walked humbly with their God, and therefore there was little cohesive community among them. The rampant injustices of court and marketplace had so polarized the people that nothing could unite or inspire them, yet they persisted in their notions of innocence and special divine favor. They thought Jerusalem would be saved, no matter what, and when Jeremiah stated plainly that this could not be, they attacked him rather then their real problems.

Of course, this is a very ancient practice—to blame the

bearer of bad tidings for the news that one brings. Centuries ago, the Greeks used to kill the messenger who brought bad news, as if what had happened was that individual's fault. And today we do a similar thing by getting mad at the newspapers and television as if they created the problems they report. This is what happened to Jeremiah. God knows he tried to warn the people, to get them "to rend their hearts and not their garments" (see Joel 2:13), but they had been heedless. Thus, when the consequences finally arrived, when it became clear that the kingdom of Judah was "sick unto death" and would be conquered, Jeremiah was abused and beaten and humiliated by the whole establishment of Jerusalem for simply acknowledging this fact—as if attacking the diagnostician could cure their cancer.

What I am saying is that part of the agony that characterized Jeremiah's life can be attributed to the awful sickness of the moment of history in which he lived. This dramatically underlines the fact that there are some eras in which it is not very pleasant to serve God! Doing God's work is by no means always a popular and affirming task. Once again, this very note was present at the moment of Jeremiah's call. He was to be God's mouthpiece, "to pluck and to break down, to destroy and to overthrow, to build and to plant."

This means that comforting and affirming are not the only forms the work of God assumes, and I am afraid we sometimes forget this as we evaluate our religious leaders. Even today, when certain sons and daughters of God disturb us and point out things about us we do not like to face, it is very tempting to seek to discredit them, to accuse them of being traitors, as many did to Jeremiah, and to seek out those who will tell us what we want to hear. This was so evident a few years ago in relation to the Civil Rights movement and the Vietnam War, and is seen today in attitudes toward church people active in providing sanctuary for refugees. Spokespersons of God in those years learned from their own wounds just how unromantic religious service can be, for it is easier to attack the bearer of bad news than to attack the causes of that bad news.

It is to Jeremiah's credit, however, that he "kept on keeping on," even when he was attacked and reviled. As deeply as it wounded his spirit, and as distasteful as he found it to have to be a person of strife, he was faithful to the word God had given him—a word that was often controversial precisely because it was so painfully true.

My conclusion, then, is that Jeremiah's roller-coaster life was partly due to his own sickness and partly due to the sickness of his times. No person who thoroughly despises himself can live peacefully through any era. At the same time, no person of God, even Isaiah, could have lived through the disintegration of Jerusalem without experiencing agony. Before Jeremiah's weeping eyes, his beloved nation came to a tragic end—its citizens deported, its monarchy demolished.

But this is not where things ended for Jeremiah. Out of his own pain and the agony of his country a magnificent hope was born—not for that day, but for what would someday emerge out of those tragic conditions. Perhaps this hope was first born within Jeremiah's own heart as he sensed what the love of God could do in changing his own self-image from despising to accepting. At any rate, as the nation was collapsing, Jeremiah was moved to do three things that set light on the other side of the darkness.

The first of these was to go to a potter's house and observe how the craftsman patiently shaped and then remade the same clay until at last he had the vessel as he wanted it. "So is Yahweh to Israel," proclaimed Jeremiah. "We are in his hands, just like clay in the hands of the potter, and those hands are hands of mercy. He will surely crush us in judgment, for we have been marred and unwilling material, but after that judgment there is still hope" (see Jer. 18:1–11). Just as Gomer was put back on the wheel of Hosea's shaping love, so Israel was still the beloved creation of a merciful God; she would not be discarded.

Jeremiah's second sacrament of hope was buying a field in the village of Anathoth just as the Babylonians were about to overrun the country. Jeremiah was a bachelor and had no need of a farm; besides, what good would the title to a piece of land in Palestine do if one was an exile in Babylon? Yet Jeremiah saw beyond the deportation and bought the field as an act of faith that "houses and fields and vineyards will again be bought in this land" (32:9)—as they were forty years later. Buying the field was Jeremiah's way of saying that Israel's sickness was serious but not fatal, for the God who once had brought her out of captivity and into this land would out of his great mercy do it all over again.

The final and greatest act of Jeremiah's hope was to write down his vision of the new covenant that he foresaw God would some day fulfill:

> Behold, the days are coming, says the Lord, when I will make a new covenant with the house of Israel and the house of Judah, not like the covenant which I made with their fathers when I took them by the hand to bring them out of the land of Egypt, my covenant which they broke, though I was their husband, says the Lord. . . . I will put my law within them, and I will write it upon their hearts; and I will be their God, and they shall be my people. And no longer shall each man teach his neighbor and each his brother, saying, "Know the Lord," for they shall all know me, from the least of them to the greatest, says the Lord; for I will forgive their iniquity, and I will remember their sin no more (31:31–34).

What we see described here is the ultimate goal of biblical religion—an internalizing of God's purposes so that they become our desire and joy. I once heard Dr. Wayne Oates use the story of Pinochio to illustrate this process. As you may remember, Pinochio was a wooden marionette who came to life, but who at first did not have his own conscience. Little Jiminy Cricket tried to function in that role, telling Pinocchio what to do and what not to do, but the only problem was that Pinochio would get away from him and into trouble. "If I could only get inside of him," Jiminy Cricket would say, "then I could be with him all the time and help him." Dr. Oates pointed out that this is the goal of personal maturing; concepts of right or wrong, which are at first external to us through our parents and society, should become internalized, so that we want to do what is right on our own.

Nothing less than this kind of relationship with him and each other is what God desires for each one of us, and Jeremiah lifts the hope that this dream will someday come true. At last the struggle will be over and the rebellion ended; we shall see God for what he is and come to love him not because we have to or are forced to, but because we want to—because our hearts flow out to him in rightful affection. The victory God's merciful persistence is striving to win is the day when we shall finally love him with all our hearts and minds and souls and strength, freely and joyfully—and that remains the greatest eschatological hope of all.

In his autobiographical novel, *Report to Greco*, Nikos Kanzantzakis tells of an earnest young man who visited a saintly old monk on Mount Athos and asked him, "Do you still wrestle with the devil, Father?" The old man answered, "Not any longer, my child; I have grown old, and he has grown old with me. He no longer has the strength . . . now I wrestle with God." "With God!" exclaimed the young man, wide-eyed. "Do you hope to win?" "Oh, no, my son," came the answer, "I hope to lose."

I submit that this kind of "losing" is precisely what Jeremiah's new covenant is all about. It means finally getting to the place where we realize that God is good and can be trusted, and where we enter the joy above all joy of saying from the heart, "Thy will be done."

It is on this hopeful note that our story of Jeremiah's troubled life comes to an end. May God grant out of our ups and downs the same hopeful vision—the hope of losing to God, that we may in so doing win eternal joy.

Questions for Thought and Discussion

1. With which Bible character discussed in this book do you most identify? Why?

2. What different experiences seem to account for Jeremiah's conflictual life?

3. Do we still tend to blame the messenger for the message? (Be specific about present-day examples.)

4. What is God's grace finally intent on doing in all of us?

5. Do you see any signs today that Jeremiah's hope of "a new heart within" is coming true for our nation? For our world? In the lives of people you know?

17

EZEKIEL
What We Can Hope For

THIS BOOK HAS BEEN an exercise in "cultivating our gift of memory" as the people of the biblical God. I have been reconstructing a portion of that background out of which our religious identity has emerged and attempting to reacquaint us with a few of those ancestors who make up our spiritual heritage. I am convinced that such an endeavor is an important one because a "person without a memory is only half a person." As Walter Shurden puts it so succinctly, "Tell me what you remember, and I will tell you who you are." In other words, the way we choose to deal with the past is a crucial factor in the shaping of both present and future.

The kinsperson on whom we now focus our attention stands at a logical dividing point in the story of our heritage. Like Samuel, the prophet Ezekiel found himself living in a "hinge era." It was his lot to experience painfully what Amos and Hosea and Isaiah had seen coming—the total demise of Israel as a nation and the agony of the Hebrews being taken into exile. As a young lad, Ezekiel grew up in Jerusalem and most probably heard Jeremiah preach, but in 598 B.C. Nebuchadnezzar came storming out of the east, and captured Jerusalem, and took Ezekiel and some ten thousand of Israel's most prominent citizens into captivity back to Babylonia. A group of them were allowed to settle at a little place called Tel-abib, on the canal Chebar that was part of an irrigation system in Mesopotamia. It was there, occupying a mud-brick hut, that Ezekiel was called to live out his days and exercise a ministry of interpretation.

One would be hard put to imagine a more difficult set of

circumstances in which to try to speak for God. Not only were these people beaten and humiliated and uprooted physically and emotionally, they were shaken down to their toes religiously because their image of God had been shattered and repudiated by the events of that day. They were experiencing something of what the Japanese went through in the 1940s when their emperor, who had been regarded as divine and indomitable, turned out to be just another human being capable of defeat.

It is bad enough when trusted friends and institutions collapse out from under you, but when your God totters, that is disillusionment indeed! Yet this is precisely what had happened to the average believer in Israel at the opening of the sixth century B.C. These folk were not only taken captive and turned into refugees far from home; they were also delivered into the abyss of despair that comes when one's God seemingly fails and the ground supporting one's altar suddenly collapses and swallows up everything. The fall of Jerusalem and the exile into Babylonia were like "the night the world ended" for the Israelites. And to this dispirited and disillusioned people the man Ezekiel—himself in exile—was called to minister.

I said earlier that Ezekiel's was a ministry of interpretation, for this is the best single word I can find to describe what he did in the transition era between life in Palestine and life in exile. Amid massive misunderstandings and false conclusions, Ezekiel set out to clarify what had really happened to Israel, what these past events meant, and what could be rightfully expected in the future. In so doing, he helped save the soul of Israel from what could have been total despair and disintegration.

Perhaps the most important interpretative task Ezekiel performed was at the point where the need was the greatest—namely, helping clarify the Israelites' image of God in terms of what he was and what role he had played in all of these events. Ezekiel made it plain that much of the disappointment that the exiles were feeling toward Yahweh was of their own making, for here, as almost always, disillusionment was the child of illusion. The reason we arrive at wrong conclusions is often that we begin from false assumptions, and this is how Ezekiel diagnosed much of Israel's religious problem.

Two erroneous ideas about Yahweh had taken root and

grown during Israel's residence in the Promised Land. One was that he was a local deity, confined to the boundaries of Palestine and living essentially in Jerusalem, especially in the temple. Those who held to this view had forgotten the fact that this Yahweh had encountered Abraham in Mesopotamia and Moses at Sinai and delivered their forefathers from Egypt. Because they had not done what we are trying to do in this book—taken time to remember who they were— they had wound up with the restricted notion that their God only resided in Palestine. From this had come the second idea that Yahweh would protect this territory and the chosen people in it no matter what might occur.

Here again, popular religion had forgotten what Yahweh's purpose in calling Israel had been and what he had wanted to accomplish out of their union. The nation had become just like a spoiled child who assumes his parents have no higher hopes than to cater to his every whim. Such a child does not attempt to understand reality or find out how history works, but presumes that he or she can go on being an infant forever, with the parent always picking up the pieces.

Such a view, of course, does not represent health, but tragic retardation. However, this is how the chosen people had come to visualize God by the sixth century B.C.—which shows how far they had gotten separated from their roots. And it is little wonder that they were devastated spiritually by the fall of Jerusalem, for what could it mean except that Yahweh was not the God they had thought him to be? He must not be as strong as he had been when he had brought them into Canaan, they reasoned. The God Marduk of the Babylonians must be more powerful, for after all, in the showdown, Yahweh had not been able to defend his home and children.

Over against this interpretation of what had happened and who God must be in light of what had happened, Ezekiel set a graphically different picture. "You have it all wrong," he cried, in effect. "You have reached an erroneous conclusion because you started from the wrong premise. Yahweh is not just a local God, confined to this and that section of the land. He is the universal Creator, the Lord of all history. And he is not just a mindless landlord with no purpose beyond defending his own territory. Yahweh is the Fulfiller of history, and he made a covenant with Israel so that they might be the first fruit of his purpose. Israel was to have been an ideal human community—a people who knew they were loved by God and were thus set free to love and serve each other rather than having to devour and use each other as other kingdoms did. They were to represent the goal toward which all history was headed under the providence of God, and thus to be a blessing to all nations.

But Israel had balked at such a cooperative venture with Yahweh. She had chosen a destiny other than the one Yahweh had given her, and this is why calamity had befallen her. The fault was not with God, as if the Holy One were too weak to defend against the Babylonians. The fault was with Israel herself, and with her rebellion against her true identity. Ezekiel pictured Yahweh's role in the fall and exile as that of Instigator, not as feeble Victim. This catastrophe was not something done to Yahweh by the Babylonians; it was something done by Yahweh to discipline Israel and call her to reality. Instead of being a sign of divine weakness, these events were the manifestation of divine strength. And needless to say, this was a radically different interpretation of those times than the popular religion of the day was making.

For twenty-two years Ezekiel hammered away at the particular interpretation of God's image which had been given him at the outset of his ministry and which continued to inform him all his days. Many people read the first chapter of Ezekiel and are confused by the bizarre figures found there. Ezekiel tells of looking up one day and seeing a storm cloud approaching filled with lightning and thunder—and in the midst of it a kind of chariot-throne. There were wheels within wheels supporting it and four-faced creatures all around, with the glory of God himself enthroned above it all.

This image at once expresses the otherness and the nearness of God. Just like Isaiah, Ezekiel realized that God is utterly beyond our capacities of comprehension. We cannot begin to get "our conceptual hands" all the way around a Mystery as vast as the Ultimate One. Yet these images also had practical significance for the particular place in history where Ezekiel found himself, for the whole vision was meant to convey overwhelming power, not weakness. The "wheels within wheels" were really two wheels set at right angles to each other, which meant God could move in any direction at will; he was mobile and not rooted to one spot. The four-faced creatures, which had a human's face in front, a lion's face on the right, an ox's face on the left, and an eagle's face in the back, stood for all the living creatures under God's control. By facing every direction, the symbols signified that God is simultaneously aware of every corner of the earth.

In short, Ezekiel's vision was a description of the same God who had come to Abraham and Isaac and Jacob in various places and times, and was Ezekiel's way of saying, "Here is what our God is really like. Our trouble all along has been that we refused to let this God be himself and have his way. He has not let us down; we have let *him* down. He has not been absent or weak or inattentive in all these calamities, but rather has been behind them in an effort to awaken us. Therefore, have done with the disillusionment that is rooted in illusions about God! He is everywhere, even here in exile with us. And his purposes are not defeated, even though we have failed him. We have come to this place by refusing to let God be himself. Let us not continue in this error, but return to his truth."

In this way, the ministry of Ezekiel illustrates that most basic transaction in history: that moment when humans, with the gods they have made, encounter the God who has made them. This is something that goes on every moment of our lives—the correcting of our image by the Image Maker himself. And I doubt whether Israel could have survived the trauma of the exile religiously had not Ezekiel clarified who God was in the midst of all this. They had so forgotten the true shape of Yahweh that they were "sitting ducks" to be disillusioned. Ezekiel's ministry was vital because he placed the blame where it really belonged—on their illusions, not God's weakness—and called them back to reality.

The other place where Ezekiel performed an interpretative task was at the point of hope. Israel had obviously expected the wrong kind of things from God; they had erroneously assumed that he would preserve Jerusalem no matter what. When this did not happen, not only the image of God but the shape of the future was called into question. And once again, Ezekiel was able to move into the vacuum to speak a clarifying word. What he did was to set out before these exiles a true hope—not a quick and easy hope, but a hope born of mercy and rooted in the fact that the God whom they had forsaken was not going to forsake them.

Ezekiel utilized three magnificent images in setting forth this hope to the Hebrew exiles. The first was the famous valley of dry bones (37:1–14). Ezekiel may well have seen a sight just like this on the trip into exile. Often the losers in an ancient war would be left unburied on a desert battlefield, and it would not be at all unusual to come up years later and find a ravine literally strewn with bleached bones. No image can possibly convey utter desolation any more graphically than this, and it must have been an accurate picture of how the exiles must have felt about their nation's fortunes. Yet in the vision God commanded Ezekiel to speak to those bones, and the prophet watched as flesh returned and life was breathed into them once more.

Here was a hope to which Israel could look forward—that the God who mysteriously and mercifully gives life in the first place is willing to give it again, even after human beings have squandered and abused it. Centuries later, St. Paul described God as the One "who gives life to the dead and calls into existence the things that do not exist" (Rom. 4:17). And this is the mystery Ezekiel sensed as he pondered the vision of the dry bones.

The functional corollary of such a vision, of course, is a sense of openness and hope toward the future. After all, if God is One who can create out of nothing and resurrect things from the dead, what is impossible? Death represents the ultimate limitation as far as we human beings are concerned, and even this boundary has been breached by God! Therefore, ultimate despair is presumptuous, says Ezekiel. Israel may appear at that moment dead and scattered like those dry bones, but Yahweh is the kind of God who knows his way out of a grave. The basis of hope is that he will give Israel life again and another chance to cooperate in his purpose. The exile is not final; there are still possibilities with a God who can make dead things come to life again.

The second vision of hope found in Ezekiel is that of a river which would begin under the altar in the new temple that was to be built when Israel returned from exile (47:1–

12). In his vision, Ezekiel watched as the river's waters flowed east through the desert, down to the Dead Sea, and made even that place of death come alive with fish and plant life. One needs only to see just how barren that terrain is to realize what a tremendous promise there is in this image. But again, it roots in the mystery of life which God is able to give and regive to his creatures. This image of the river is to the natural order what that of the resurrection of the dry bones was to human beings; it represented the coming of vitality to places of deadness, even to places of faraway exile!

The tenderest hope image of all, however, is Ezekiel's picture of Yahweh himself becoming Israel's shepherd and seeking out those who have strayed away and gotten lost (34:1–31). Ezekiel condemns the leaders across the years who should have shepherded Israel more faithfully but who did not care enough about the people to protect or feed them. But the time will come, he says, when Yahweh himself will assume this task; he will "ask after" each sheep and proceed to seek and to save those who have gotten lost. This is the image, of course, that Jesus picked up and used in defining his own task. And think what it must have meant to the Hebrew exiles in Ezekiel's time to hear that they were not forgotten or abandoned, but would someday be sought and gathered back by the Lord himself when they had learned their lesson.

This is a word every one of us longs to hear in our lostness and "beaten-downness"—that we are not abandoned or forgotten, that we still matter to our Maker. Ezekiel's image of God as shepherd says this and promises that, like a shepherd seeking for the one lost sheep, the Lord God is seeking each one of us. What a comforting consolation!

What Ezekiel does in these three images is to say the two things about God that would have to be true if there is any ultimate hope—one, that he is able to work with sinners and to redeem them; and two, that he is willing to do so. If he possessed the power but was not interested in saving us, or if he were intent on saving us but not able to do so, there would be no hope. However, Ezekiel put both of these qualities together to present a picture of an Almighty One who is merciful and a Merciful One who is almighty. And that image serves as a fitting climax to this journey of glad reunion with some of our spiritual forebears. Who can help but hope when all creation is finally held in the tender embrace of such a One?

Questions for Thought and Discussion

1. How did Ezekiel shift the perspective for the Hebrews of his day?

2. Do you know anyone today who you feel has a ministry of interpretation?

3. What are some false assumptions about God that are prevalent today and that could lead to religious disillusionment?

4. Identify the various images Ezekiel used in his interpretative task?

5. What are the evidences today that Ezekiel's vision of God was true?